Ideas and Methodologies in Historical Research

This book explores the versatile nature of historical methodology and its use in interdisciplinary research. Based on the historical overview of the appearance of one sort of historical ideas and disappearance of another, the book aims to demonstrate a wide range of possibilities of research in the field and to show how the pursuit of historical truth may facilitate the formation of collective memory and how the application of research tools can explain events in the contemporary world.

Vladimer Luarsabishvili is a Professor of the School of Politics and Diplomacy at New Vision University. He has founded a book series *Rethinking Society. Individuals, Culture and Migration* (NVU Press, 2020) and edited *Rethinking Mamardashvili. Philosophical Perspectives, Analytical Insights* (Leiden, Brill, 2022).

Routledge Approaches to History

45 Family History and Historians in Australia and New Zealand
Related Histories
Edited by Malcolm Allbrook and Sophie Scott-Brown

46 Writing Russia
The Discursive Construction of AnOther Nation
Melissa-Ellen Dowling

47 How to Write About the Holocaust
The Postmodern Theory of History in Praxis
Theodor Pelekanidis

48 The Politics of Time in China and Japan
Back to the Future
Viren Murthy

49 Nation and the Writing of History in China and Britain, 1880–1930
Asier H. Aguirresarobe

50 Ideas and Methodologies in Historical Research
Vladimer Luarsabishvili

51 Clarifying the Past
Understanding Historical Commissions in Conflicted and Divided Societies
Cira Palli-Asperó

For more information about this series, please visit: https://www.routledge.com/Routledge-Approaches-to-History/book-series/RSHISTHRY

Ideas and Methodologies in Historical Research

Vladimer Luarsabishvili

Routledge
Taylor & Francis Group
NEW YORK AND LONDON

First published 2023
by Routledge
605 Third Avenue, New York, NY 10158

and by Routledge
4 Park Square, Milton Park, Abingdon, Oxon, OX14 4RN

Routledge is an imprint of the Taylor & Francis Group, an informa business

© 2023 Vladimer Luarsabishvili

The right of Vladimer Luarsabishvili to be identified as author of this work has been asserted in accordance with sections 77 and 78 of the Copyright, Designs and Patents Act 1988.

All rights reserved. No part of this book may be reprinted or reproduced or utilised in any form or by any electronic, mechanical, or other means, now known or hereafter invented, including photocopying and recording, or in any information storage or retrieval system, without permission in writing from the publishers.

Trademark notice: Product or corporate names may be trademarks or registered trademarks, and are used only for identification and explanation without intent to infringe.

Library of Congress Cataloging-in-Publication Data
A catalog record for this title has been requested

ISBN: 978-1-032-28404-0 (hbk)
ISBN: 978-1-032-28408-8 (pbk)
ISBN: 978-1-003-29673-7 (ebk)

DOI: 10.4324/9781003296737

Typeset in Times New Roman
by codeMantra

To my father

Contents

	Acknowledgments	ix
	Introduction	1
1	Methods and theories of historical studies	6
2	Historical past	20
3	Structuralism and post-structuralism	23
4	Memory studies. Social amnesia	27
5	Archive as an institution of active memory	36
6	Postmemory and Ectopic Literature	42
7	History as literature, narrative and practice	57
8	Microhistory	64
	Conclusion	70
	Index	77

Acknowledgments

This short book on ideas and methodologies in historical research is a humble act of gratitude to all those who had helped to form my understanding of history and its role and importance for today and tomorrow. My former colleagues from the Archive of the Ministry of Internal Affairs of Georgia, as well as from the Institute of National Remembrance of Poland provided inspiration to plan, elaborate, and shape this work. The members of editorial and advisory editorial boards of the book series *Rethinking Society. Individuals, Culture and Migration* (of which I am an editor since its foundation in 2020), together with authors who published their texts in its volumes, contributed enormously to my interdisciplinary approach to history. My very special thanks go to my students – both in Georgia and Chile – for fruitful academic communication. And finally – my gratitude to colleagues at Taylor and Francis/Routledge and to an anonymous reviewer, which made possible the publication of this book.

Introduction

This book is a kind of methodological summary of scientific articles, which were published by me in 2013–2019. Initially, my basic idea was to conduct research in different fields of science, including history, literature, philosophy, translation, and rhetoric. However, with time, the work done prepared a fertile ground for the formation of a research set of instruments that could be used for historical investigation. The mentioned can be explained by two factors: the first one is a methodological need, which is a basis of all scientific research; the other one is the importance of history for historical and non-historical studies. The contribution and significance of historical context in literature, philosophy, translation, rhetoric, and other fields of research are obvious. In addition, I got interested in the history of the Soviet Union in general and of the Georgian SSR in particular. My interest was inspired by five fascinating years which I spent working in the Archive of the Ministry of Interior of Georgia (former KGB archive), where along with my colleagues I studied and published materials preserved in the archives of three Soviet bodies: The State Security Committee, the Central Committee of the Communist Party, and the Ministry of Internal Affairs of the Georgian SSR. Our studies were reflected in the articles[1] and monographs.[2] An interdisciplinary modern approach to research (which means the simultaneous use of methodological instruments of different sciences), as well as the use of historical examples as arguments in the process of working on lecture themes delivered by me at different universities of Georgia, Spain, and Chile, conditioned me to think of separating and classifying historical ideas and theories, which could be helpful for explaining of the development of consciousness in different epochs. That is how I decided to compose this book, which would be interesting to both the researchers and, especially, students. Reading it, students will study history as

2   *Introduction*

a science on the one hand, and as a methodological instrument in the process of interdisciplinary research on the other.

In this book, the term 'history' has two different meanings: the first refers to a time period that combines past events, and the other – to a science that studies past events. From this perspective, a historian is a professional whose object of study is historical, and not philosophical, literary, rhetorical, or other kind of knowledge. If we acknowledge the idea of historical knowledge, we must rely on the concepts such as historical past, historical fact, historical reality, or truth when studying history. The process of historical reconstruction is also of paramount importance, as it means a gradual restoration of events that have historical significance (which distinguishes them from other, non-historical events) on the one hand, and is based on the existence of historical facts on the other. Conclusively, we have two types of challenges. These are: (1) What kind of events can be considered historical facts? (2) What is the role of a scientist in the process of reconstructing historical events?

Sources used in historical research by a historian can be of two types: primary and secondary. Primary sources include archival documents, letters, diaries, personal papers, government documents and decrees, photo, radio and TV-related materials, films, e-mails, and blogs. Technical progress enriched historical research with materials available on the Internet. One of the important primary sources are oral histories told by participants in historical events.[3]

Secondary sources are created by historians based on the usage of primary sources. It includes articles and books describing past events. However, the usage of secondary sources is as important as of primary ones, since a historian begins a research project after studying historiography or written histories conducted by his predecessors, especially when it comes to the history of history as a science. In conclusion, history is not a static but rather a dynamic science that constantly offers new interpretations, discoveries, and discussions. Moreover, historical conclusions may be changed because of raising a question differently, as well as gaining additional facts, making a new appraisal, or changing cultural values of society.

A question of the role of researcher in the process of historical research is discussed in the first chapter of the book and includes aspects of subjectivity and non-biasedness of scientific inquiry. This is a bridge that connects the past with the present, and particularly with modern public and political processes, and to a certain

Introduction 3

extent, determines the near future of society. Restoring the desired version of history, or historian's bias toward past events, and 'the issue of social amnesia' is a reality, which reflects values established in society on the one hand, and criteria for nations' attitude and appraisal of history on the other.

The book consists of eight chapters. Although in most cases each subsequent chapter is an evolutionary development of the ideas offered in the preceding chapter, their content and sequence are not based on the chronological principle. Among them are chapters discussing structuralism and non-structuralism, describing memory and post-memory. The first chapter offers features of historical discourse, subjectivity, and ideology, which may be or may not be subordinated to the chronological features.

In conclusion, we can assume that chronology is an important, though not the only, factor in studying historical ideas and methodologies. Furthermore, the chronology, or the study of the sequence of historical facts or events, can't be the only determinant factor in studying history as a science. The most important factor is the historical context in which certain ideas are formulated and developed or lost. Historical context is a broad concept and includes terms and meanings like past, historical past, fact, truth, or reality. The study of the above-mentioned features became a basis of the table of contents of this book, and therefore, for its ideological and methodological construction.

Another feature that was considered when creating the table of contents is that every chapter, except one, is based on ideas developed by a particular scientist or group of scholars, which were from the beginning historical (e.g., the views of M. Oakeshott or representatives of the Italian School of Microhistory), or non-historical (e.g., ideas of structuralism and post-structuralism).

The fifth chapter, which is not based on concrete authors' ideas, is an exception. It offers a review of the archive as an institution of active memory. Although this chapter reflects cultural and historical ideas, as well as some aspects of their development, it highlights the contribution of the archive to the process of historical reconstruction.

The first chapter offers an overview of the general objectives of the methodology, as well as the normative rules of various scientific fields, and types of their construction. This chapter also describes methods and theories of historical research, as well as three types of historical methods, historical epistemology, Rankean empiricism, and the New History, historical methodology, post-empiricism,

4 Introduction

and post-positivism. The conclusive part of the chapter offers a brief discussion on historical discourse, as well as issues concerning a historian's subjectivity and ideology.

The second chapter is an attempt to observe the characteristics of the historical past and its constituents. It is based on the works of M. Oakeshott and lists the basic terminology, which was used by the scholar, while trying to explain history as the essence of science, and to place it alongside other sciences.

The third chapter provides a brief overview of the features of structuralism and post-structuralism, and their contribution to the development of the historical science. The works of several scholars will be briefly mentioned in it.

The fourth chapter offers issues concerning memory studies and social amnesia.

The fifth chapter describes the essence of the archive and its contribution to the process of the reconstruction of history, highlighting the historian's role in the functioning of the archive, as well as in the process of understanding the nation's identity and cultural values.

The sixth chapter describes the role of post-memory and ectopic literature in the study of history on the example of the Main Administration of Soviet prisoner-of-war camps and colonies.

The seventh chapter can be divided into three parts. The first part offers an overview of history as literature and is based on the works of Hayden White; the second one connects history with narrative and is based on Paul Ricoeur's studies; and the third one describes history as a practice based on the ideas of Michel de Certeau.

The eighth chapter is concerned with microhistory, and its representatives of the Italian School.

Notes

1 Luarsabishvili, V., Tushurashvili, O. 'Materiály o okupaci Československa v roce 1968 v archive Ministerstva vnitre Gruzie', *Securitas imperii,* 24, 01, 2014, pp. 180–202; Dżachua I., Luarsabishvili, V., Tushurashvili, O., 'Archiwum MSW Gruzji – przeszłość, teraźniejszość i przyszłość', *Przegląd Archiwalny,* 8, 2015, pp. 91–108; Tushurashvili, O., Luarsabishvili, V., 'The Great Terror in Georgian SSR: Documents and Reflection', *Annales Universitatis Mariae Curie-Skłodowska,* LXX, 2015, pp. 29–60; Luarsabishvili, V., 'A brief history of the Great Terror in Georgia', *Revista de historia actual,* 14–15, 2017, pp. 75–183; Luarsabishvili, V., Tushurashvili, O., 'Archiv Ministerstva vnitre Gruzie', *Securitas imperii,* 31, 2, 2017, pp. 234–251; Luarsabishvili, V., 'Wydarzenia marca 1956 r. oraz początek gruzińskiego ruchu dysydenckiego', in

Kutkowski, A., Piątkowski, S., Lublin-Warszawa (eds.), *Miasta buntu w imperium sowieckim. Konteksty radomskiego Czerwca 1976 roku*, 2020, pp. 197–202; and Luarsabishvili, V., 'Los campos soviéticos para prisioneros de guerra en la RSS de Georgia (1945–1954)', *Cuadernos de Historia Contemporánea*, 43, 2021, pp. 227–252.
2 *The Dissident Movement in Czechoslovakia and Georgia (A Brief Overview)*, Tbilisi: Archive of the Ministry of Internal Affairs, 2013; O. Tushurashvili, V. Luarsabishvili, *The History of the Dissident Movement in Georgia* (Tbilisi: Archive of the Ministry of Internal Affairs, 2016); *Wielki Terror w Sowieckiej Gruzji 1937–1938. Represje Wobec Polaków* (Warszawa-Tbilisi: Instytut Pamięci Narodowej, Komisja Ścigania Zbrodni Przeciwko Narodowi Polskiemu, 2016); *The Occupation of Georgia through the Lens of the Bolsheviks (1921)* (Tbilisi: Archive of the Ministry of Internal Affairs, 2016); *Farewell, Brothers! We are being Executed Tonight!* (Tbilisi: Archive of the Ministry of Internal Affairs, 2016); *Большой террор в Абхазии (Абхазская АССР): 1937–1938 гг.* (Тбилиси: Архив Министерства внутренних дел Грузии, 2017г.); *The Occupation of Georgia. Bolshevik Interpretations (1921)* (Tbilisi: Archive of the Ministry of Internal Affairs, 2017); 9 April (Tbilisi: Archive of the Ministry of Internal Affairs, 2017); *The Soviet Repression of Poles in the Georgian SSR during the Great Purges (1937–1938)* (Series: Poles in Georgia – Georgians in Poland, Tbilisi-Warsaw, 2019).
3 Oral History Association: https://www.oralhistory.org/

Bibliography

Kramer, L. S., 'Literature, criticism, and historical imagination: The literary challenge of Hayden White and Dominick LaCapra', in Hunt, L. (ed.), *The New Cultural History*, Berkley and Los Angeles: University of California Press, 1989, pp. 97–128.
Tosh, J., *The Pursuit of History: Aims, Methods & New Directions in the Study of Modern History*, New York: Longman, 1991.
Trachtenberg, M., *The Craft of International History: A Guide to Method*, Princeton, NJ: Princeton University Press, 2006.
Wolf, Jacqueline H., 'Historical methods', *Journal of Human Lactation*, 34, 2, 2018, pp. 282–284.

1 Methods and theories of historical studies

1.1 Objective of Methodology. Specialized Normative Rules and Types of Their Reconstruction

The objective of any methodology is the rational reconstruction of specialized normative rules. Unlike a method of historical reconstruction, it implies the possibility of revealing specialized features through the logical and empirical justification of reconstruction. This view is idealized to some extent because the reality, along with rationality, is determined by factors such as power and privilege. The specialized methodology differs from irrational factors and aims to restore the cognitive criteria and ideals, on the basis of which the specialists in the field evaluate each other's scientific findings and examine its quality. Therefore, the methodology allows the existence of basic cognitive agreement among researchers in the field. This applies to both the Humanities and Life Sciences.

Along with the basic ideals of truth, the methodology restores other cognitive ideals like the ideals explaining the field and the indicators of its development. That is how methodological differences are identified for those who recognize the unity of the scientific method and for those who are pro dualism. The question arises: Is there a single explanatory ideal for all fields? This question has been a subject of debate since the 1950s and is known as the difference between explanation and understanding in special literature. In the 19th century, classical mechanics was considered a paradigm for all fields of science, including history. It was believed that the fields differed only in the development phase. This means that they were characterized by scientific maturity or immaturity. History fell into the latter category.

Since the 19th century, the significance of historical methods and theories has been a subject of dispute in the circle of historical science. It happened between 1880 and 1920, and between 1965 and 1985. This was caused by three factors: history was formed as an independent scientific discipline, historical thinking came to a deadlock, and the public interest in history increased.

Following the formation of history as an independent scientific discipline, it acquired a characteristic form of academic fields, and its functions were determined. Its major objective was to create 'objective knowledge' about the past. This resulted in the development of opposing methods and theories. Individual historians and schools of history tried to create the golden mean, which would enable to reconstruct history with the greatest possible accuracy. This brought historical thinking to a deadlock.

Among the causes of disagreement and misunderstanding were issues such as a historian's objectivity and bias, the contribution of documents and other materials to the process of historical study, and ideology as a bridge between the objectivity of a researcher and the selection of research material.

History as the newly formed scientific field attracted the public attention due to the aforementioned reasons. It became not only a space uniting the past and the present, but also a precondition for defining the future. Past events seemed to continue into the present and became an integral part of the future action plan. In social and political respect, history created models of behavior and action, revised established cultural values, and established modern and at the same time historical context to cultivate new values. Thus, history laid the foundation for the development of modern sciences such as politics (including foreign), sociology, economics, and psychology.

1.2 Methods and Theories of Historical Studies

When discussing theory within the framework of historical science, history can be considered as an event, and as a knowledge related to this event. Therefore, they will have different theories, which (a) characterize history as a practical field or process (e.g., Marx's historical theory of class conflict), and (b) reflect features of historical knowledge (e.g., scientific knowledge in history). The theories of the first category can be called material theories, and the second – cognitive theories, or reflecting of historical knowledge. The latter includes epistemological and methodological theories.

8 Methods and theories of historical studies

Noteworthy is that material and cognitive theories are interrelated. On the one hand, according to the material theories, historical process is characterized by its determining regulated mechanism, and links to cognitive theories, according to which, true knowledge of history means knowledge of general laws. On the other hand, material theories mean nonregulated mechanisms, which are linked to cognitive theories, according to which, true knowledge of history is knowledge of concrete facts and not general laws.

As regards the term 'historical method', it was coined in the 16th century by Jean Bodin, who tried to ascertain if it was possible to restore past events on the basis of a contrasting study of sources.[1] The objective of the historical method was to annul skeptical beliefs related to the possibility of acquiring knowledge about the past. At that time intersubjective method emerged, which replaced an ancient belief regarding the issues of a historian's impartiality, truth, and trust. In the 18th century, historians of the Enlightenment period (including August Ludwig Schlözer) acknowledged the unification of historical research and its textual presentation to the public as the historical method, and not a critical assessment of sources. This model has its roots in the rhetorical tradition, and in 1970 it returned to historical research. One of the initiators of its return was a theorist of the history of Germany Johann Gustav Droysen. In the 19th century, the historical method was developed by the German Historical School, and particularly by Leopold von Ranke and Barthold Georg Niebuhr. Their 'new approach' was a return to the past – they saw methodologies as a critical analysis of sources. They thought that the creation and presentation of the historical text belonged to literature and thus, categorized them as aesthetic components.

In the 19th century, sciences were developed as separate fields, based on their separate research methodologies. This was considered to be the key to 'truth' and 'objectivity'. For example, sociology was equipped with sociological methodology, and history – with historical one.[2,3]

In the 19th century, the historical method was based on the study of written sources and was developed into a three-step technique. These were: (a) finding relevant sources, (b) critical analysis of sources or a technique, which determined the origin of sources in both time and space, as well as their authentic nature, and (c) interpretation of sources that were a description of events that really took place.

There were two types of critical analysis. These were: internal and external. Internal analysis meant a textual study of sources, or a criticism of the hermeneutic processes by means of which texts were created (if it was presented in an incomplete or multi-version form), as well of those textual features, which determine the issues concerning authorship and textual authenticity. External analysis meant checking of sources by the materials obtained from other sources. In this regard, supplementary sciences, including paleography, toponymy, chronology, numismatics, diplomacy, and sphragistics were significant. External analysis was particularly valuable during the study of the ancient period. As regard a modern research of history, supplementary sciences were replaced by archeology and anthropology during the study of non-literate, oral, or a lack of source cultures. In the 20th century, the use of multiple methodologies within the framework of one field became admitted, and since the 1960s, it was a norm. This resulted in raising an issue of dividing sciences and establishing their borders. Some scientists considered a poly-paradigmatic nature of research to be a sign of crisis. In the 1960s–1970s, that affected the science of history too. Therefore, historical methodology was divided into quantitative, biographical, comparative, typical, causal, discourse, microhistorical, and psychoanalytical analysis.

1.3 Historical Epistemology and Historical Methodology. Rankean Empiricism and the New History

Historical method and historical theory can be linked on two levels. These are: epistemology and methodology.

Historical epistemology refers to a theory of historical knowledge – historical sources, foundations, etc. In the 19th century, there were two epistemological approaches: empiricism and anti-empiricist idealism.

A historian studies the state of mind (ideas and actions) in the past, or its distant manifestation in time and space. That is the difference between empiricist and non-empiricist approaches. While according to the empiricist approach, the state of mind can be studied by means of empirically visible epiphenomenon, anti-empiricism (phenomenological and hermeneutical views) studies the state of mind by means of non-empiricism (phenomenology uses introspective methods, and according to hermeneutics, reading others' minds are like reading texts).

10 Methods and theories of historical studies

While according to empirical theories, observation of objects is a cognitive activity, hermeneutics believes that a cognitive activity is an interpretation of meaningful symbols, as well as an interpretation of symbolically structured phenomena (e.g., events and objects of culture). These opposing views, which were formed during 1850–1970, were criticized in the 1980s by postmodern theorists.

The role of theory in orthodox professional historiography is immense. Within its framework, history is a practical activity of the field. Empiricism (or the theory that knowledge is gained through induction by means of sensory experience or visual evidence, and that it corresponds to reality) incorporates several theoretical approaches such as positivism (according to which, historical process, as well as the natural sciences subject to laws or generalization), historicism (according to which, every historical period is unique, and their study must be based on that factor), and humanism (according to which, the subject of history is a human-being and his unchangeable nature). These theories have their own history, which was gathered in the works of German scientist Leopold von Ranke, who was deemed to be an organizer of historical empiricism.

Rankean empiricism opposed with Hegelian philosophical historicism, according to which history had idealistic nature, as an expression of the implementation of the transcendental idea of the historical society. According to Hegel, a historian was a man of his own time, carrying modern ideas of his context; he was equipped with established categories, within the framework of which, he contemplated and discussed historical events.

Unlike Hegel, von Ranke proposed a kind of historical knowledge that would be based on documentary material, as well as detailed scrutiny of historical facts, which actually happened, taking into account that each historical period has its own unique characteristics. At the same time, each period would be consistently linked to its following era, which would lead to a unified understanding of history, or to a linear process, which would connect past with present. According to von Ranke, history was distinguished from philosophy, for it consisted of specifics and facts, and not of general and abstract. However, he noted that history was not based on specifics and facts alone. In his opinion, from detailed scrutiny of the fact of particular events the historian should move toward a 'universal view', identifying their unity and larger significance, ultimately contributing to the construction of a world history embodied in the progress.

Leopold von Ranke's views contributed greatly to the development of historical science. His ideas were particularly prevalent in the USA and the UK. In the universities of North America, he was deemed to be an architect of scientific history, and in the UK the empirical method, or the process of reconstruction of history based on documentary sources became a prior historical method. Historical education at the universities of Oxford and Cambridge was based on the empirical method. Rankean approach to the study of history is still relevant today. For this reason, objective and archival research based on evidence gained advantage in the process of Holocaust studies.

In spite of the aforementioned, Rankean approach was not acceptable to all historians. American scientist Charles Beard pointed to the role of interpretation in the process of reconstructing history. In addition, Michel Foucault and Gayatri Spivak disagreed with Rankean approach in respect of the linear development of history.

1.3.1 Historical Methodology

In this period, views on historical methodology like epistemology were divided into two. While according to the first view, the scientific method had a unified nature, the other one recognized the dual nature of the methodology.

Adherents of the dual methodological approach noted that the historical explanation differed from the acknowledged model not only empirically, but also logically. Based on the abovementioned, methodological dualism was formed in three forms. These were: ontological, epistemological, and methodological forms.

An ontological argument was first systematically developed by Johann Gustav Droysen, and later by Robin Collingwood and his school. Their views emerged from Giambattista Vico's and Hegel's doctrine, which was based on the idea of identity of subject and object in history: people interact with one another in historic space. Therefore, history is an autobiography of human beings. History is the process, within the framework of which, people express and develop themselves in the form of different cultures, and due to the fact that history is their doing, people can directly perceive it like the writer who composes an autobiography. Historians try to reconstruct those cultures and concrete ideas, which are revealed in cultural practice (religious, rituals). Besides, they study material artifacts (churches and religious items). When the historian explains the past, he establishes contact between culture and the ideas expressed in it. When this is implemented successfully, the historian describes the phenomenon. Understanding of history is akin to understanding text. However, historical texts are more or less lost and therefore, they need to be reconstructed based on the trace left by them. For this reason, understanding of history is based on the relation between ideas, and their time and space context. It is implementable by moving to the past and joining all components with the integral. Therefore, understanding of history logically will be different from other scientific disciplines: the form of connections presented by historians is not causally determined and can't be formed based on the general laws. Historical connections are not necessary but possible laws, which may always differ from their modern form. They are based on faith-based and not empirical findings, as well as critical study of sources and similar arguments. Understanding history constructs possible, not true or discovered knowledge. Since it depends on the historian's ability of interpretation, which is learnt and not formalized, historical understanding is subjective, or entrenched in the historian's culture, time, and space. In this respect, one of the works of Gadamer is noteworthy.[4]

The second form of methodological dualism is epistemological. It was first developed by Wilhelm Dilthey. It is also related to Hegel's ideas. However, W. Dilthey related his views not to the relationship between subjectivity and objectivity, but to the 'internal experience' of historical facts, as 'mental fact'. Mental facts of history consist of feelings, thoughts, and achievements of people living in the past. W. Dilthey also recognized Johann Gustav Droysen's views related to the relationship between time and space and denies causal arguments similar to laws. However, unlike to J. G. Droysen, the scientist emphasized the difference between 'internal' and 'external' experiences as the foundation for methodological dualism.

The third form of methodological dualism is methodological. It is non-ontological because it does not share the view according to which, history studies the object, which fundamentally differs from the nature, and is not epistemological (historical fact differs from natural fact). This type of methodology was developed by Wilhelm Windelband, Heinrich Rickert, and Max Weber. According to them, there were two ways of knowledge or methodological approach. They were related to two fundamentally different goals, or interest in knowledge. The first one was generalization method, when object was departed from a particularity, and revealed its general characteristics. According to W. Windelband, the natural sciences were characterized by the generalization method. The other goal was the method of divergence when a historian departed from the general and described concrete characteristics. According to W. Windelband, ideological sciences, including history, were characterized by this method.

1.3.2 The New History, or the Annales School

The New History is a kind of historical research, which is written using traditional, or paradigmatic, or Rankean methods' antipodes. The term 'New History' was coined by French scientists Jacques Le Goff and Pierre Nora. Differences between traditional and new approaches to historical research can be subsumed under seven categories. These are:

1 According to the traditional paradigm, history is associated with politics. Politics, in turn, is associated with the state, and thus, history is more national and international rather than a local phenomenon.
2 While followers of the traditional approach view history as a narrative of events, for the creators of the new history, history is associated with structural analysis.
3 The traditional historical approach has always been concerned with historically significant individuals and their lives (e.g., government officials, generals, and religious figures), and the rest of society had less role in the historical context.
4 According to the traditional paradigm, history was written based on the documents – one of von Ranke's most successful discoveries was to reduce the role of narrative in historical discourse and to increase the significance of documentary sources.
5 The traditional paradigm didn't consider the historian's ability of asking multiple questions.
6 According to the traditional paradigm, history is an objective event. The historian is tasked with giving information concerning a fact to the reader or describing an event, which happened.
7 According to the traditional paradigm, history is the field of actions for professionals.

14 *Methods and theories of historical studies*

The New History is associated with Lucien Febvre and Marc Bloch. In 1929, they founded the journal *The Annales* that was to contribute to the development and dissemination of their ideas. Marc Bloch believed that a historical event should be explained by the context of both modern and past events. During their evaluation, increased psychological interval, which will be resulted from technical progress should be considered. According to M. Bloch, the technological advances like electricity or air travel made the modern man departed from his ancestors, and there were only writings that helped generations to keep close. Texts were carriers of information between chronologically distant generations, which at the same time indicated the continuation of civilization. The scientist believed that historical figures should be studied in their own context, in their mental atmosphere, in space of thinking, which is not a part of our modernity. According to M. Bloch, misperception of the present was caused by neglecting the past, and at the same time, the misperception of the present was not an instrument for studying the past. The scientist considered that the basic research ability of the historian was to perceive the living being. Therefore, M. Bloch didn't approve historians' research, which was based on the chronological study of events. He offered to read history backward or to proceed from the known to the unknown. The scientist believed that the documents concerning past events were not always comprehensive. This means that the more departed is the epoch from us, the less knowledge we have of it. The past is reality, which won't change. However, the knowledge of the past can constantly be changed and refined. In addition, the past treats researchers hostile, and allows to study what the past itself offers.

Noteworthy is the fact that not only representatives of the Annales school opposed Rankean approach to historical research. In the 1930s, scientists Lewis Bernstein Namier and Richard Henry Tawney didn't approve narrative way of reflecting historical events in the UK. In 1900, Karl Lamprecht disagreed with the traditional paradigmatic approach in Germany. L. Febvre and M. Bloch's predecessors who gathered around French sociologist and intellectual Émile Durkheim didn't share Rankean principles (They published the journal called *Année Sociologique*, which was an ideological predecessor of *The Annales*).

1.4 Post-empiricism and Post-positivism

Post-empiricism abandoned the idea that scientific knowledge could be grounded on a sensory experience. The ideas that the Life

Sciences were based on established knowledge and the Humanities were based on possible knowledge were revised. According to the new idea, any kind of sensory knowledge was formed and realized by means of concepts and theories. As any kind of empirical knowledge was based on interpretation, it could be reinterpreted. Thus, during the period of post-empiricism, the boundary between subjective (based on interpretation) and objective (based on empirical observation and experimentation) knowledge was removed. On the one hand, post-empiricism relativized the difference between theoretical and empirical knowledge, and, on the other, separated the types of interpretive and empirical knowledge from one another. The methodology of all scientific disciplines was based on the principles of conceptualization and interpretation. Humanities and Life Sciences became equal in respect of research. Their scientific objective became empirical argumentation and intersubjectivity.

Post-positivism, which was based on post-empiricism, abandoned the idea that all scientific explanations could be subsumed under one model. Therefore, the views on the methodological homogeneity of the Life Sciences and Humanities were diverged. Post-empiricism and post-positivism formed a new view concerning the nature of historical knowledge in the postmodern era and revived the role of literary theory in the process of development of historical science. The relationship between history, rhetoric, and literature was rediscovered, which caused to increase attention to the linguistic forms in the process of historical representation. Historical theory and method became associated with aesthetics, rhetoric, and politics.

1.5 Historical Discourse

The formation of historical discourse is different from the formation of any other kinds of discourse. This difference is due to the fact that historical discourse is made of two kinds of material – 'the true story', or what happened (probably) in the past, and the relationship between the story (past) and modernity. In the process of formation, historical discourse is filled with fictional structures. This is a two-stage process. In result, we get a historical narrative formed by the imagination. As if on cue, the issue concerning subjectivity of the historian arises.

What is subjectivity and how is it related to mistrust of historical facts? How important is the narrative's role in the formation of historical discourse? What connection is between historical reconstruction on the one hand, and ideology and politics on the other? The answers to these questions can be particularly important in respect of the formation of national and universal historical discourse.

Traditionally, professional objectivity meant the historian's impartial independence to events. The shift from objectivity to subjectivity, or in other words, bias can be viewed in three historical phases: the ancient historian's main duty was to describe and classify facts without declaring his own position. In the modern era, this has been changed. In the second half of the 19th century, Homer's impartiality and Thucydides' objectivity stopped existing, and historical stories were accompanied by the historian's explanations. According to Hayden White, in the early 19th century, history had an opportunity to become a science by breaking the connection between the historiography and rhetoric. As if on cue, the issue of mistrust in historical discourse arises when a professional narrative is formed with the help of imagination.

As regards the ideology, this issue has been studied by many scientists. Among them noteworthy are the works by Antonio Gramsci, Louis Althusser, Slavoj Žižek, Terry Eagleton, Michael Billig, and Jorge Larrain. However, I would like to draw your attention to T. van Dijk's idea of the relation between ideology and discourse.

T. van Dijk explains the ideology as social representations shared by a social group, which is the organizational basis of political groups. As soon as ideology becomes part of politics, it establishes itself in political discourse. According to van Dijk, the ideology reflected in the discourse is explicit and formulated.

For the formation of the ideology, it is important to know the stages of the development of the ideas' history, which forms a philosophical basis of public consciousness. Consciousness is formed based on the experience that the individual gains in life, or the ideas, which s/he gets ready, and later transforms and makes them acceptable. From centuries past, man had an idea of the arrangement of the world and the identification of himself with it. This idea changed over time. The world was perceived differently in different periods. E.g., in the early stage of the development of philosophical thinking, the world existed independently of man. Later, based on the ideas cultivated by Hegel and some historians, the notion of ideology was discussed from a historical perspective. The main reason for this was the dominance of social-political considerations in the world of ideas. The historical perspective was greatly influenced by an epochal event such as the French revolution. It revived and personified the role of history in the formation of ideas. The view, which unified the general and abstract world was transformed into a more specific event, defined by national character, which had been the result of less philosophical and more global impact. Finally, the idea of people (nation) was replaced by the idea of class, according to which the structure of society depended on the relationship between social classes. This is how the ideological system of defining classes was established.

The described evolution of the structure of ideas connected community members to the concept of consciousness and, at the same time, made possible the division of society into classes.

At first the notion of 'ideology' didn't have an ontological significance, and it referred to the theory of ideas alone, without having a direct relationship with the system of values. In France, its adherents were philosophers who, like to the French philosopher Etienne Bonnot de Condillac, rejected metaphysical perception of the world and based their study of culture on anthropological and psychological essentials. The modern conception of ideology was emerged when Emperor Napoleon discovered that these philosophers opposed to his imperial ambitions and called them 'ideologists'. Since the 19th century, the term has been widely adopted. Later it was used by the leaders of the proletariat. Methodological formation of the notion of 'ideology' took place within the framework of Marxist theory. This emphasized the existence of classes and their interests in the system of thought. It was followed using the notion from the economic perspective, which made the ideology a part of reality, or life. Today this approach, which in the past was a privilege of sociologists, is used by different political systems. In Germany, the initiators of the mentioned were Max Weber, Werner Sombart, and Ernst Troeltsch.

Notes

1 Jean Bodin, *Methodus ad facilem historiarium cognitionem*, Parisiis: Martinum Juvenem, 1566.
2 E. Bernheim, *Lehrbuch der historischen Methode: mit Nachweis der wichtigsten Quellen und Hülfsmittel zum Studium der Geschichte*, Leipzig: Dunker &Humblot, 1889.
3 Ch. Langlois and Ch. Seignobos, *Introduction aux études historiques*, Paris: Éditions des archives contemporaines, 1987.
4 Gadamer, Hans-Georg, *Truth and Method*, London and New York: Continuum, 2004.

18 *Methods and theories of historical studies*

Bibliography

Ankersmit F. R., Kellner, H. (eds.), *A New Philosophy of History*, Chicago, IL and London: University of Chicago Press and Reaktion Books, 1995.
Appleby, J., Hunt, L., Jacob, M., *Telling the Truth about History*, New York: Norton, 1994.
Arendt, H., 'The concept of history', in Arendt, H. (ed.), *Between Past and Future: Eight Exercises in Political Thought*, New York: Viking Press, 1961, pp. 41–90.
Barthes, R., *The Rustle of Language*, Berkley and Los Angeles: University of California Press, 1989.
Burke, P., 'Overture. The new history: its past and its future', in Burke, P. (ed.), *New Perspectives on Historical Writing*, Cambridge: Polity Press, 2001, pp. 1–24.
Droysen, J.-G., *Historik*, Stuttgart: Frommann-Holzboog, 1977.
Evans, R., *Telling Lies about Hitler*, London: Verso, 2002.
Fay, B., Pomper, P., Vann, R. (eds.), *History and Theory. Contemporary Readings*, Malden, MA: Blackwell Publishers, 1998.
Gardiner, P. (ed.), *Theories of History: Readings from Classical and Contemporary Sources*, New York: The Free Press, 1959.
Gay, P., *Style in History*, New York: W.W. Norton & Co, 1974.
Goodman, N., *Ways of Worldmaking*, Indianapoli, IN: Hackett Publishing Company, 1978.
Gunn, S., *History and Cultural Theory*, Harlow: Pearson Longman, 2006.
Hausmann, T., *Erklären und Ferstehen. Zur Theorie und Pragmatik der Geschichtswissenschaft*, Frankfurt am Main: Suhrkamp Taschenbuch Verlag, 1991.
Hegel, G. W. F., *Lectures on the Philosophy of History*, New York: Dover Press, 1956.
Iggers, G., *Historiography in the Twentieth Century. From Scientific Objectivity to the Postmodern Challenge*, Hannover; London: Wesleyan University Press, 1997.
Mannheim, K., *Ideology and Utopia. An Introduction to the Sociology of Knowledge*, San Diego, CA: A Harvest Book, 2015.
Megill, A. (ed.), *Rethinking Objectivity*, Durham, NC: Duke University Press, 1994.
Novick, P., *That Noble Dream: The Objectivity Question and the American Historical Profession*, Cambridge: Cambridge University Press, 1988.
Oexle, O.-G. (ed.), *Naturwissenschaft, Geisteswissenschaft, Kulturwissenschaft; Einheit-Gegenzatz-Komplemetarität?* Göttingen: Wallstein, 1998.
Rorty, R., 'Philosophy and the mirror of nature', *Philosophy*, 56, 217, 1979, pp. 427–429.
Soffer, R., *Discipline and Power: The University, History and the Making of an English Elite, 1870–1930*, Stanford, CA: Stanford University Press, 1994.

Stern, F., *The Varieties of History: From Voltaire to the Present*, London: Macmillan, 1970.
Van Dijk, T. A. (2006) 'Politics, ideology, and discourse', in Brown, K.(ed), *The Encyclopedia of language and linguistics*, Oxford; New York: Pergamon Press, Vol. 9, pp. 728–740.
White, H., *Metahistory. The Historical Imagination in Nineteenth Century Europe*, Baltimore, MD: John Hopkins University Press, 1973.
White, H., 'The question of narrative in contemporary historical theory', *History and Theory*, 23, 1, 1984, pp. 1–33.
White, H., *The Practical Past*, Evanston, IL: Northwestern University Press, 2014.

2 Historical past

The question of the historical past isn't easy. Moreover, in some respects, it is confusing to produce a syntagma like the 'historical past'. According to Keith Jenkins, while something happened in the past, and the past is dead, the history is a result of historians' work. Historians study past events, and with chronology in mind create a text called historical discourse. The newly created discourse becomes a historical domain, which has subjective and fragmented nature.

The fact that the historical past is created by the field professionals (historians) doesn't make it easy to understand. In order to understand and perceive this notion better, it is necessary to distinguish it from the notion of 'practical' past. The latter is the result of our personal, daily life experience, as noted by political philosopher Michael Oakeshott.

Discussing history, M. Oakeshott distinguished several terms, including 'historical past', 'practical past', 'historical fact', 'historical truth', and 'historical reality'. Let's briefly review each of them.

M. Oakeshott's desire – to distinguish 'historical' from 'practical' past, emphasized the historian's professional obligation: when he formed his conclusions, he guided with the ideas, which were based on the need of research topic and not of personal. According to the scientist, the historian's objective approach to the 'historical past' would be different from practical considerations in that (a) while practical perceptions may or may not always be considered to have historical nature, historical approach with any additional features will always be an integral part of the past; (b) while in the practical approach, indicators are used to predict the future, and the time structure is 'present-future', in history the present is always considered as 'recorded past', which must be understood historically, and its time structure is 'present-past'. M. Oakeshott does not regard the 'practical past' as an enemy of humanity but discusses it as an enemy of history.

The 'historical past' is not past per se. It is different from personally memorized or mythical past. The scientist thinks that the biggest confusion is that the 'historical past' is considered the 'practical past', for the past reflected within the 'practical past' does not have historical significance.

The 'practical past' emerges when somebody uses the past to explain and justify modern events, e.g., when a political figure relies on past events to reinforce belief in his own political program.

In addition, M. Oakeshott distinguishes the historical past from the so-called 'contemplative past' and notes that the latter's place is in historical novels. In other words, he does not identify the notion of aesthetic with the notion of the scientific past. He thinks that the historical past is always in the present time, and at the same time, historical experience is always presented as the past. M. Oakeshott believed that this contradictory situation is a feature of historical ideas.

The term 'historical fact' is what is gained by experience. It is not a given fact. An event is a fact when it gains a place in the world of ideas. As regards the history, historical fact means the conclusion, outcome, or discussion, which belongs to the world of modern experience.

The term 'historical truth' refers to something that is satisfying within a historical experience, which is coherent in the world of historical ideas. The truth of a particular fact depends on the coherence of all the facts. Within historical experience, there is no absolute data that are protected from changing. Every element reinforces the other element. Facts come from the past (written sources, eyewitness memories, etc.), but they do not exist in isolation. The 'historical truth' is based on a historical fact that is an object of judgment or construction.

Finally, let's review the term 'historical reality'. In historical experience, reality is events (e.g., the fall of Bastille), institutions (e.g., the Roman Empire), and persons. M. Oakeshott calls them 'historical individuals'. On the one hand, history does not create historical individuals, and, on the other hand, history is based on the concept of individuality.

Bibliography

Isaaks, S., *The Politics and Philosophy of Michael Oakeshott*, London and New York: Routledge, 2006.
Jenkins, K., *Re-thinking History*, London and New York: Routledge, 2003.

Nardin, T., *The Philosophy of Michael Oakeshott*, Philadelphia: Pennsylvania University Press, 2001.
Oakeshott, M., *Experience and Its Modes*, Cambridge: Cambridge University Press, 1958.
Oakeshott, M., *On History and Other Essays*, Oxford: Basil Blackwell, 1983.
Oakeshott, M., *Rationalism in Politics and Other Essays*, Indianapolis, IN: Liberty Press, 1991.
White, H., *The Practical Past*, Evanston, IL: Northwestern University Press, 2014.

3 Structuralism and post-structuralism

3.1 Structuralism

The derivation and development of structuralist ideas are related to the names of French anthropologist Claude Lévi-Strauss, Russian literary critic Roman Jacobson, and Swiss linguist Ferdinand de Saussure. The core of their ideas was the independence of significance from the individual and literary form, and its dependence on the language system or structure. In 1945, this view was widely developed in France, and covered scientific disciplines such as anthropology and Marxist political theory. Structuralism was widely regarded as the ability to define objective conditions that could form the foundation for, as well as explain, the phenomena under observation, including culture, literary text, and social systems. In post-war France, structuralism was a type of thinking that reflected the individual's attitude to the world (as it happened in the case of Sartre's phenomenology), and the role of classes in the development of history (within Hegelian Marxism). For structuralists, individuals and classes represented systemic or structural events rather than historical subjects or forms. They thought that historicism and humanism were events, which had some responsibility for the wars and genocides of Europe during the first half of the 20th century.

For structuralists, language became a model for describing phenomena like communication and cultural and social organization. Language became an instrument for the study of culture, social and economic systems. In addition, structuralist deemed that the mechanisms by which these systems operate act unconsciously, or they are left beyond the consciousness of the individuals or groups. This approach greatly weakened the human factor and its role in the functioning of different systems. Afterward, components of the system (linguistic, cultural, public) were discussed relatively

DOI: 10.4324/9781003296737-4

(considering their relationship with other components) rather than dynamically (taking into account their development over time). This weakened and denied the importance of historical depth and process.

In the 1960s, French structuralism became increasingly influential. It covered Marxist theory, and particularly the works of L. Althusser. His Marxist ideas, expressed in various papers [*For Marx* (1959) and *Lenin and Philosophy* (1971)] reflected and at the same time developed the ideas of French structuralism. He used linguistic ideas as methodological instruments for the study of society. Among them was the discussion of economic relations as a language structure, within which social systems acted as components of the structure, not hierarchical or causal connections. Based on structuralist ideas, L. Althusser emphasized that culture, as well as ideology creates forms of human consciousness and action. The ideology thus became the individual's imaginative relation to the living conditions, and what made him individual. The ideology makes the individual act within such organized living spheres such as religion, education, family, and the media. L. Althusser called their unity the 'state ideological apparatus'.

Structuralism affected both French and foreign scientists of the next generation. Next-generation scholars of French structuralism, including Michel Foucault and Pierre Bourdieu, based on the works of Gaston Bachelard and Georges Canguilhem, shared structuralist approaches within historical science. These scholars viewed history as a sequence of 'discoveries' and focused not on scientific achievements and facts, but on their epistemological characteristics in a particular historical period.

Claude Lévi-Strauss's ideas were shared by representatives of Anglo-American cultural anthropology (which was called 'social anthropology' in the British area). Particularly noteworthy is the influence of his ideas on the views of Clifford Geertz and Mary Douglas.

3.2 Post-structuralism

According to the title, post-structuralism is a movement that has developed chronologically after structuralism and is its critique. There are two main ideological differences between these two movements. The differences distinguish post-structuralism from history. The first is an absolute rejection of the notion of 'system' regardless of language, culture, and society. The other is the determination of the unsustainable nature of *meaning*. While Saussure thought that the *meaning* had linguistic nature and binary opposition, post-structuralist philosophers, including Jacques Derrida thought that the *meaning* was not the notion of fixed features. J. Derrida considered the meaning, which was formed by means of language, to be not only binary, but also multifaceted. In his opinion, words acquired meaning with the help of other words, which were not only of the opposite meaning. At the same time, the meaning varied depending on the linguistic context. Therefore, the language was kaleidoscopic rather than a stable structure. To illustrate the changing nature of representation, J. Derrida introduced the definition of 'difference', which consists of two parts: one is 'differ', which denotes difference, and the other 'defer', which denotes infinity of meaning. Based on the above, as well as more on written word that uttered one, J. Derrida identified 'deconstruction', as a reading strategy. While the past was presented to him only as a textual form, history as a corpus of texts was presented as a phenomenon of stable features, which contradicted the historian's attempt to interpret it. Language, culture, and society as systems are the objects of observation and not abstract ones for the post-structuralists. Language and culture are open systems, and they don't imply all possible forms of meaning or action alone.

Despite this difference, post-structuralism shared several ideas on which structuralism is based, including the fact that history is not united and the sum of the linear development of events, as well as the fact that language is assigned a meaning as a source of *meanings* ('discourse', by M. Foucault's terminology, or a group of formulations, which belong to separate systems: economic discourse, psychological discourse, etc.). Therefore, it is difficult to draw a sharp boundary between these two movements. M. Foucault is a philosopher of both movements. However, in the 1960s, he didn't approve the fact that he was deemed to be a structuralist. In addition, the term post-structuralism is more of Anglo-American than French derivation.

As regard the impact of structuralism and post-structuralism on the development of different fields of sciences, the impact of post-structuralism was greater historically. In the 1970s, this covered historical science too. In France, post-structuralist ideas were developed in the works of Pierre Bourdieu, and in North America – in the texts of historical philosophy and intellectual history by Hayden White and Dominick LaCapra. In Britain, the echo of ideas was reflected in Althusser's Marxist views. Finally,

26 Structuralism and post-structuralism

post-structuralism was interesting for the formation of feminist ideas, which was emphasized in the works by Hélène Cixous and Judith Butler.

Bibliography

Dosse, F., *History of Structuralism: Volume I: The Rising Sign, 1945–1966*, Minneapolis: University of Minnesota Press, 1997.
Dosse, F., *History of Structuralism: Volume II: The Sign Sets, 1967–Present*, Minneapolis: University of Minnesota Press, 1997.
Gunn, S., *History and Cultural Theory*, Harlow: Pearson Longman, 2006.
Kurzweil, K., *The Age of Structuralism: From Lévi-Strauss to Foucault*, New Brunswick, NJ: Transaction Publishers, 1996.
Sarup, M., *An Introductory Guide to Post-structuralism and Postmodernism*, Harlow: Harvester Wheatsheaf, 1993.

4 Memory studies. Social amnesia

4.1 History and Memory

The relationship between 'history' and 'memory' has been the subject of debate among scientists for a long time. This dispute is particularly observable in France, where these two notions have opposite meanings. While history is written and authoritative phenomenon created by state institutions, memory is oral, plural, regional, minority-dominated, and always closely related to identity. In the context of modern historical research, scientists can't ignore memory studies because they are interested in studies related to the 'historical truth', as well as in aspects of regional, religious, and sexual minorities. The study of collective memory is extremely significant for the study of the history of society, and particular of its tragic papers. These include Holocaust and Gulag studies, as well as Armenian Genocide and other similar issues. In this regard, the historian's profession even acquired a new, legal aspect – historians became involved in the processes of the trial as experts of restoring 'historical truth', as it happened in the course of the Nazi trials of the French occupation.

In the study of memory issues, Patrick Geary noted that the debate on history and memory gained particular momentum in France, which may have been due to some social and cultural violence experienced in many other countries (Nazi Germany, the effects of the Vietnam War on the USA, etc.).[1]

History divides the sequence of events into epochs, periods, wars, and revolutions. Memory creates connections between past events and the present. While history records changes, collective memory makes a certain image of groups like family, church, and nation. Mass culture and electronic media, as modern bearers of memory, change their structure. According to Andreas Huyssen, technological media affects the sense of time and memory, and changes our

DOI: 10.4324/9781003296737-5

perception of their nature. The increased speed of dissemination of information changes the ability to perceive the past and removes its boundary between present and future.

As a result of the mentioned, the history of memory – a special branch of historical research was created. In his works, Guenther Roth developed the notions of 'memory interests', 'memory conflict', 'memory hegemony, 'memory adaptation', and others. In his opinion, the history of memory was not created by historians, but rather it was created in the course of history and lasted until members of society remembered it. In this process, the historian acted as a mediator for the society which made decision either to accept or to reject his interpretation. Consequently, if a historian or an expert wrote history for another expert or the historian, it would not be resulted in the creation of the history of memory. The history of memory would develop when ideas were progressed beyond historians and recognized by members of society. This was particularly evident in the writing of the history of nations over the last two centuries. Ernest Renan noted that nation is a collection of memories. This is how history emerges as a phenomenon of more than individual memory, which must be transmitted to be accepted. Therefore, it is not the historian who creates history alone – literature, media, festival, sport, and other phenomena, which Michael Billig calls 'banal nationalism' (including hoisting the national flag on the roof), create national histories.

Guenther Roth views a nation as an abstract unity of memory, which spans long historical periods and encompasses the entire society. He distinguishes two types of memory: society memory that is rich in experience, which can only exist in the modern generation, and the other that is beyond the modern generation but does not cover the entire society, e.g., confessional groups, whose ideas are based on a particular version of history and is different from the ideas of other confessional groups.

According to Johann Martin Chladni, a nature of history is based on the perception of its eyewitnesses and can never be perceived unambiguously. He thought that historical knowledge was based on the observation and memory of individuals, as well as what individuals talked about with others, what they learnt from others (Jan Assmann calls it 'communicative memory'). Chladni thought that this kind of history could not be changed by subsequent generations. Eyewitnesses are the guarantor of the transmission of the true history. If there are no more eyewitnesses, Chladni calls this kind of history 'ancient history'. The scientist also distinguishes eyewitnesses from those who have not seen historical events themselves. For him, memory is not an instrument for historical research, but history itself is a part of historical memory. It is completely based on the experience of eyewitnesses or is created by means of transmission from eyewitnesses to the others.

John Harold Plumb distinguishes between 'past' and 'history'. He uses the term 'past' to describe historical events, which are mobilized for a specific purpose – it is done since ancient times in accordance with social demand, when people use the past to explain their origin or objectives of their lives, as well as to justify the work of state institutions, to give moral examples, to revive cultural and educational processes, to interpret future, and explain the function of the nation. The idea of the 'past' has always been related to the future and will probably remain like that.[2]

As regard the notion of 'history', it is different from the notion of 'past'. Its task is to create scientific information. It is an intellectual phenomenon. According to H. Plumb, history as a science has a destructive nature. It breaks the system of poetic significance that humans construct by means of the 'past'. According to the scientist, the aim of the historian as a scientist is to free people's history from the tyranny of the past, which facilitates to use past to explain the present.

Putting the historical memory within the framework of historical science is related to the works of Reinhart Koselleck. The scientist identifies three types of history writing and associates them with three fragments of time that are unchangeable since the time of Herodotus and Thucydides: short-, medium- and long-lived experiences. The stories of eyewitnesses are part of collective or communicative memory, as well as parts of all three categories. It passes on to the next generations. It is an act of an innovative nature. When historical science shifted from the study of events to the analysis of long-standing structures, it moved away from the innovative form. As regards the next two categories, one of them is defined as the ordinary activity of the historian and implies a coherent nature of history, which is referred to as historical narrative. When that feeling disappears, history must be rewritten, which is the highest type of the innovative approach, possible within the context of historical science. This is possible in times of crisis and is acceptable to the public. Society accepts it because its new explanation requires a new view of history.[3]

In the 19th century, the people (Volk) or the nation became a new orienting point for the center of political events and the system of social values. The democratic concept denoting the nation was promising in terms of future development, and at the same time it provided a new explanation for the phenomenon of the past. It gave a new color to history, according to which all history could be represented in national form. This new rewriting of history was based on the myths of the founding of nations. Therefore, history and the past were not regarded as phenomena of opposite significance. History became a decisive factor in the formation of nations, and in the nationalization of daily life, as well as in the formation of nation-states. This became possible in the 19th century, which was based on the involvement of people (as a component of the past) and of history in the process of an authentic scientific field. It was very important for history to elevate this field to the level of science because in the 19th century fields of sciences were formed as cult systems. This interrelationship between history and the past is described in detail in the works of Paul Ricoeur, who does not distinguish them from one another and gives it a reciprocal significance. In his opinion, they depend on one another. The scientist believes that history can influence the past only in combination with memory. He calls this effect 'therapeutic': historical memory as historical therapy.

4.2 Collective Memory: The Works of M. Halbwachs

The introduction of the term 'collective memory' into scientific circles is related to the works of Maurice Halbwachs. He indicates the dissemination of individual memory among certain groups and means, by which the group constructs and presents its own past. Based on the ideas of Henri Bergson and Émile Durkheim (about internal and objective time and society as a form of sociological analysis and collective consciousness), M. Halbwachs focused on memory as a social form of mediation and a mean of reflecting individual experience. É. Durkheim discussed collective representation within the framework of religion and culture and paid little attention to remembering of common past by members of society. The main idea that he developed in his essay 'The Elementary Forms of Religious Life' (1912) is the role of ritual in the process of social cohesion, according to which, religious rituals and symbols preserve shared experiences and reinforce collective identity – rituals provide a representational function of society over time.

A. Bergson considered memory as a personal and subjective experience, in contrast to M. Halbwachs, who studied the social frameworks within which individuals remember, and within which memory concerning the past is related to everyday life. According to M. Halbwachs, individual memory depends on social context or environment. He notes that individual memory can't exist without words and ideas, which are instruments, which are not invented by individuals although they are used in their living environment. Thus, the expression 'collective memory' does not refer to a single, monolithic form of memory, but rather indicates the existence of collective memory as there are collective groups. M. Halbwachs does not agree with the idea of mythical collective consciousness and places memory within a particular group. According to him, there is no universal memory, because every collective memory requires the existence of groups in space and time. Since memory is related to a group, there are as many memories as there are families, religious organizations, ethnicities, or nations that associate their own group with a common past.

Unlike autobiographical memory, which is related to individual experiences shared by other people, collective memory is connected to social institutions and is conditioned by indirect participation or observation of memorable events. Collective memory is a memory of the past, which is significant for a certain group of people with a common past. M. Halbwachs believes that collective memory is a socially formed concept, not a given one. Memory is not a simple reflection of information or facts from the past, but an imaginative activity, which combines subjective impressions and meanings. According to M. Halbwachs, individual memory, which is quite different from collective memory, is unreasonable generalization, because any memory is a precondition for the development of society and is bound by social institutions and habits. Individuals, as members of a group, remember the event because they share language and culture, and their memories of the past events are formed through their participation in specific groups, including family, school, religious institutions, cities, and ethnic groups. M. Halbwachs believed that language as well as systems of social nature enable to reconstruct the past. Collective memory forms the basis of the collective identity of a particular group. M. Halbwachs considered that belief, interest, and desire create a desirable past at the present. For instance, in the German context, national and social memory was connected to social and cultural changes and ideological differences between East and West. Collective memory is the existence of a social feeling among the groups whose experiences and modern interpretations of the past make a solid foundation for their unity. According to the scientist, memory can't be neutral or individual because it is caused and transmitted by social institutions such as schools, museums, and national holidays. M. Halbwachs emphasizes the existence of the imaginative and restorative capacity of memory, noting that the act of remembering has an interpretative nature, enables to construct content, and is not objective in its essence.

According to M. Halbwachs, collective memory has a generative nature – as soon as the event is beyond the present, it becomes a part of history. In the German context, the generative nature of memory is particularly significant – people of the war generation, who were born with the national and socialism ideas are no longer alive, and their memory acts indirectly, by means of books, museums, documents, films, and narration.

4.3 Individual Memory: The Works of Jan Assmann

Contrary to the notion of 'collective memory' derived from M. Halbwachs, German sociologist Jan Assmann offers the concepts of 'communicative memory' and 'cultural memory'. J. Assmann identifies M. Halbwachs' 'collective memory' with 'communicative memory' because it is the memory of everyday interaction and the way of existence of oral history. Communicative memory has a generational nature and lasts for maximum 100 years. Afterward, it is forgotten. Cultural memory has an objective nature and is developed by social institutions. While it has an indirect nature, communicative memory has direct nature. Cultural memory is preserved through texts, rites, and monuments.

Jan Assmann's influence is enormous both in Germany and in other countries. In Germany and France, his ideas were adapted to medieval historical studies conducted by Otto Gerhard Oexle. Studies in this area have contributed much to the study of monastic and funeral rites. In 2003, German and French scientists published their mutual work on the issues of collective memory in the period of Late Medieval and Early Revival.[4]

4.4 Social Memory and Social Amnesia

In the 1970s–1980s, sociologists paid special attention to the work of M. Halbwachs, published in 1925.[5] In result, social memory became an object of interest of both cultural and literary studies, as well as for their adjacent fields.[6] Sociologists defined social

Memory studies. Social amnesia 33

memory as non-paradigmatic and transdisciplinary.[7] It is studied during reviewing the issues concerning identity, multiculturalism, orientalism, and imperial domination. Postmodernist scientists associate social memory with concepts of objectivity, truth, and narrative. For historians, it is an important instrument to represent the past and give a modern meaning to it.

Human life experience is multifaceted. Experience creates an individual's attitude to the past, which is perceived as narrative, and has a historical significance. For this reason, describing experience is one of the most difficult aspects of historical research. Converting it in narrative form is a precondition for the public to remember its own history. Memory narratives enable to pass on, understand, document, repeat, and use history for various purposes.

Social memory makes the existence of both the individual and the collective legal. Its narration and repetition enhance the possibility of self-realization of society and the nation. The thing that is historical truth will become the basis of its identity like individual memory, which defines and forms the basis for the existence of the individual.

The concept of forgetting or social amnesia is closely related to the abovementioned issues. The creation and comprehension of dominant narratives are important for the formation of social memory. Its additional manifestations are ceremonies, monuments, memorials, and similar phenomena, which form social memory. They sometimes have more effect than historical narratives. They have the function of social identification, which is based on the selective understanding of the past. Unlike the narrative, they don't enable to exist alternative reality and establish individual connections with selected events of the past, often without any consideration. The thing, which is not remembered or accented, is doomed to forget. Consequently, the past can be changed as if it was done by society itself.

Anthropologists of some cultures view collective forgetting as a crucial step called ethnographical memory. Closing archives and similar institutions facilitate the formation of social amnesia and create barriers for assessing the past. The past is lost for those who didn't experience it personally. Amnesia is easy to achieve, for there is nothing in the individual memory opposite to the suggested reality, and there is nothing preserved (or accessible) in the archives.

It is possible that in respect of politics social amnesia may be benevolent, for it is used to connect members of society or to incite nostalgic feelings at present. However, types of forgetting, which are aggressive and intend to destroy historical evidence can't be useful for the development of society. An example of this is to call the victim an enemy to legitimize the actions of the state repressive apparatus. Within the framework of social memory, this may be called 'enemy syndrome', which emerged during the Balkan wars in the 1990s, when ethnic cleansing received social and cultural legitimacy due to undocumented past conflict, because documents proving opposite circumstances were deliberately destroyed.

Notes

1 Patrick Geary, *Phantoms of Remembrance: Memory and Oblivion at the End of the First Millennium* (Princeton, NJ: Princeton University Press, 1994).
2 Herald Plumb, *The Death of the Past* (London: Palgrave Macmillan, 1969).
3 Reinhart Koselleck, 'Enfahrungswandel und Methodenwechsel. Eine historisch-antropologische Skize', in *Zeitschichten. Studien zur Historik* (Frankfurt am Main: Suhrkamp, 2002, pp. 27–77).
4 Hanno Brand, Pierre Monnet, *Martial Staub (Hg.): Memoria, Communitas, Civitas. Mémoire et conscience urbaines en occident à la fin du Moyen Âge* (Ostfildern: Thorbecke, 2003).
5 *Les cadres sociaux de la mémoire* (Paris: Presses Universitaires de France, 1952), originally published in *Les Travaux de L'Année Sociologique* (Paris: F. Alcan, 1925).
6 Mary Douglas, 'Introduction: Maurice Halbwachs [1877–1941]', in M. Halbwachs (ed.), *The Collective Memory* (New York: Harper and Row, 1980). Patrick H. Hutton, 'Maurice Halbwachs as historian of collective memory', in *History as an Art of Memory*, University of Vermont, 1993.
7 Jeffrey Olick, Joyce Robbice, 'Social memory studies: from 'collective memory' to the historical sociology of mnemonic practices', *Annual Review of Sociology*, 24, 1998, pp. 105–140.

Bibliography

Blouin, F. X. Jr., Rosenberg, W. G., *Processing the Past. Contesting Authority in History and the Archives*, New York: Oxford University Press, 2011.
Kattago, S., *The Nazi Past and German National Identity*, Westport, CT: Praeger, 2001.
Langewiesche, D., 'Memory history and the standartization of history', in Paletschek, S. (ed.), Popular Historiographies in the 19th and 20th Centuries: Cultural Meanings, Social Practices, NED-New Edition, 1, New York: Berghahn Books, 2011, pp. 121–139.

Levy, J. F., 'Acrostics as copyright protection in the Franco-Italian epic: implications for memory theory', in Brenner, E., Cohen, M., Franklin-Brown, M. (eds.), *Memory and Commemoration in Medieval Culture*, London and New York: Routledge, 2013, pp. 196–217.

Schmitt, J.-C., 'Images and the work of memory, with special reference to the six-century Mosaics of Ravenna, Italy', in Brenner, E., Cohen, M., Franklin-Brown, M. (eds.), *Memory and Commemoration in Medieval Culture*, London and New York: Routledge, 2013, pp. 14–32.

5 Archive as an institution of active memory

5.1 Archives: History and Development

There is no doubt that the ancient Jews had some ideas about the archive. Let's appeal to history to testify this: Noah decided to bury the documents in the ground before the deluge myth to gather them again later. Besides, by this time there was an archive, which preserved documents in Canaan. One of the definitions of the word 'sepher' is 'city of archives'. Chroniclers and writers often referred to the existence of archives in their works in the Chaldean Assyrian period in Egypt, as well as in Persia and Phoenicia. For example, the Egyptian priest and historian Manetho personally read various laws and expressions that were engraved on the high columns and capitals. The Jewish priest Ezra mentioned the archives in the city of Babylon in his writings.

As regards the civil archives, its history dates to the Roman Empire, when the politician and military leader Julius Capitoline constructed the 'Tabularium', where documents were preserved. Later the Roman emperor Antonius Pius created archivist occupation. The word 'archivum' is derived from the Greek 'archeion' and refers to the place where documents were created and stored.

There are three periods in the development of the archive as an institution. These are: *pre-archival* (from antiquity to the 19th century), *development* (from the second half of the 19th century to the second half of the 20th century),[1] and *modern* (from the second half of the 20th century to the present). Theoretical approaches were not developed during the organization of archives in the pre-archival period. It was practical, or functional approach to the realization of specific archival tasks. In the development period, Archival Studies was formed and separated from other disciplines as a separate field, and in 1898, a special textbook was published.[2] In 1922, 1928, and 1956 important monographs were published on the subject.[3]

DOI: 10.4324/9781003296737-6

From the second half of the 20th century, special literature was accumulated in the field of Archival Studies, which studied it from a historical, academic, and practical perspectives.[4]

Archival studies is a discipline of the modern social sciences and thus encompasses culture, history, and philosophy. They are, on the one hand, based on classical academic works (such as those of Hannah Arendt, Jacques Derrida, and Michel Foucault) and on the other, on modern scientific studies, when the field of archival research is becoming more and more expended and gets in the center of modern and topical scientific interests. We will discuss this issue in the following subchapter.

5.2 Archive as a Part of History and Culture

Modern historical research is often conducted within the framework of cultural research. In particular, studies devoted to archives and memory emphasize two types of cultural memory: *active* and *passive*. The institutions of active memory preserve the past as present, while the institutions of passive memory preserve the past as past. History (along with religion and art) is one of the core areas of active cultural memory, which can be recovered in two ways: through the presentation of sacred texts, artistic masterpieces, or key historic events; and thanks to the storing of documents and artifacts from the past. The first of these is implemented in history textbooks, which Charles Ingrao appropriately termed 'weapons of mass instruction';[5] the second is through institutions such as archives. Accordingly, archival publications are an important instrument for historical research in the scope of society, as archival studies combine the two aforementioned approaches. On the one hand, publishing archival materials makes them accessible, and, on the other hand, these archival materials themselves may comprise an important part of history textbooks.

Historians and researchers work on archival documents, which – once they are published – lose their archival status and acquire the status of historical documents. Therefore, they participate in the process of creating national memory. For this reason, it is not surprising that archives have always belonged to institutions of power: the state, the police, the law, and the church. Time, however, quickly overwhelms these archives. The archival documents become part of history and only historians and researchers are interested in archival depositories. We must therefore distinguish between *political archives* and *historical archives*.

It is particularly important to study those historical archives which preserve documents related to the activities of various state and law enforcement structures (political parties, the police, and security structures). The documents classified 'Secret' and 'Top Secret', based on the legislation of a specific country, may be preserved in archives for a long period of time.[6] After a given period, the documents may be declassified and thus become accessible to the public. Archives created under totalitarian regimes are extremely significant, both historically and politically. As a rule, such non-democratic regimes keep most of their documents classified. Only after the death of a dictator or a change in the state regime for other reasons are archives declassified and preserved documents become accessible for consultation.[7] History can then be reviewed and studied again using archival materials. From the early 20th century historians and social scientists took an interest in the issue of how the public perceives criminal acts committed by governments, as well as by individual state functionaries and officials. A nation's readiness to reflect on its past objectively is a significant component in the formation of a democratic and civic society. In this sense, publishing archival materials is particularly important. This is the task of archival employees who are neither scientists nor researchers. Although archival publications lacking expert commentary do not reflect a scientific attitude toward history, the publication of unabridged documents preserved in archives (with only brief descriptions, glossaries, and annotations needed to decode abbreviations) is a significant tool to evaluate the past objectively. The following subchapter offers a review of the scientific study of archival records or the work conducted by a historian in the archives.

5.3 The Role of Historian in Archives

The historian's work in archives is based on the goals that s/he has set. The historian may be just a simple observer, a professional who is studying history with no specific objective, or the historian may seek to reevaluate and rework history.

Documents found in the archives can be both primary and secondary. In both cases, the aim of the historian is 'historization', or to help the documents regain their lost relevance. Documents lose relevance when they abandon *political archives* and enter the new context of *historical archives*. The relevance of archival documents affects not only the importance of the scientific and educational value of the institution but serves as an effective tool for the reevaluation of the past and for creating new historical approaches to the development of national memory as well.

Both employees and historians working in archives conduct difficult systematic research to analyze history. Very often the materials preserved in archives shed light on the history not only of the country in which they are held but on that of other countries as well. Moreover, the history of one country is often restored based on the archival materials preserved in the archives of other countries. It is especially important to examine totalitarian states when the central administration sends circulars and orders to the different republics which constitute the state (e.g., as in the case of Soviet Georgia). Aside from the Soviet regime, the Fascist and Nazi state systems also exerted influence over conquered lands.

Unlike ancient and medieval history, the study of a country's contemporary history is important not only for the creation and restoration of national memory, but also for the consolidation of the political and social system of the country.

The archive, as an *institution of active memory*, is not only a repository of documents, but also an effective institution for the reconstruction, interpretation, and understanding of the history of the country. Both primary and secondary documents can contribute much to the creation of a new historical reality, which is a necessary precondition for the formation of national memory.

Archival research is an effective instrument for international cooperation that helps to bring different cultures closer. Employees of the archives, as well as historians of different countries, create modern scientific discourse, which is a subject of multifaceted and diverse interpretation in the cultural, philosophical, and historical contexts.

For the democratic development of the country, which implies scientific and political pluralism in the formation of society, the interpretations of 'new' historical reality based on archival documents are necessary conditions for understanding the nation's identity and values in a modern multifunctional and tolerant environment. Therefore, archives are necessary for further development not only in a particular country, but also on a universal scale.

Notes

1 This period is mentioned differently in the special literature. Some authors call it dominant (Cook, 1997), while others call it classical (Thomassen, 1999). Eugenio Casanova distinguishes four periods of

archival development: from antiquity to the 13th century, from the 13th century to the 14th century, from the 14th century to the 18th century, and from the 19th century to the 20th century (Casanova, 1928).
2 Muller, S., Feith, J. A., Fruin, R., *Handleiding voor het Ordenen en Beschrijven van Archieven* (Groningen: Erven B. Van der Kamp, 2d ed., 1920). The textbook consists of six parts: the first describes the origin and composition of archival funds, the second part discusses the issue of storing documents in the archives, the third expresses opinions on archival descriptions, the fourth one deals with inventory, the fifth – additional issues concerning descriptions, and the sixth discusses terminology. The textbook was translated into several languages, including German (1905), Italian (1908), French (1910), English (1940), and Portuguese (1960).
3 Jenkinson, H., *Manual of Archive Administration* (Oxford: Clarendon Press, 1922); Casanova, E., *Archivística* (Siena: Lazzeri, 1928); Schellenberg, T., *Modern Archives: Principles and Techniques* (Chicago, IL: University of Chicago Press, 1956).
4 *Archives in the ancient world* (Cambridge, MA: Harvard University Press, 1972), by Ernst Posner is very important in this respect.
5 Noteworthy is his work 'Weapons of mass instruction: schoolbooks and democratization in Central Europe', *Contexts: The Journal of Educational Media, Memory and Society* (New York & Oxford: Berghahn, 2008, pp. 199–209); 'Democracy and dissolution: macedonia and the fate of Yugoslavia', in Jovanović, D. (ed.), *Makedonija i Sosedite* (Skopje: Cyril and Methodius University Press, 2009); 'Western intervention in Bosnia: operation deliberate force', in Elleman, B. (ed.), *Naval Coalition Warfare: From the Napoleonic Wars to Operation Iraqi Freedom*, London: Routledge, 2010, pp. 169–82.
6 For example, the operative correspondence of the Soviet state security organs was packed based on a special regulation. Namely, special terms were used. These were: series 'К'– Top Secret/Extremely Urgent, letter 'А' – Secret/Urgent/, letter 'Б' – Non-secret/Urgent/ and letter 'В' – Secret/Not-urgent/. All these terms, except the letter 'Б' were to be placed at the top right-hand corner and a special signature confirmed with the seal of coat of arms appeared beneath. Besides, these parcels were to be sewed up in the middle and sealed up. If it was impossible to sew up a parcel, it was sealed up in five places: One seal was put in the middle and the other four in the corners.
7 Under nondemocratic regimes governments periodically destroy materials that are preserved in their archives, often to conceal evidence of state crimes. For example, in 1948 the then Minister of Security of Georgia, Nikoloz Rukhadze, destroyed archival-investigation cases against former employees of the Ministry of Security in the Security Archive. Officially these documents were declared to be non-operational and hence unimportant (MIA Archive, f. 6, c. 5519, v. 2, p. 231). In addition, between 1956 and 1988, based on orders passed by the regime, around 2 million operative documents were destroyed in the Security Archive of Poland. Later, in 1989, several further orders were issued on the destruction of operational cases, which caused the reorganization of the Ministry of Internal Affairs.

Bibliography

Assmann, A., 'Canon and archive', in Erll, A., Nünning, A. (eds.), *A Companion to Cultural Memory Studies*, Berlin/New York: Walter de Gruyter, 2010, pp. 97–107.

Casanova, E., *Archivística*, Italia: Lazzeri, 1928.

Cook, T., 'What is past is prologue: a history of archival ideas since 1898, and the future', *Archivaria*, 43, 1997, pp. 17–63.

Escobar Escobar, H., 'Origen e historia de los archivos', *Boletín Cultural y Bibliográfico*, 5, 4, 1962, pp. 440–447.

Kingman, E., 'Los usos ambiguous del archivo, la Historia y la memoria', *Íconos. Revista de Ciencias Sociales*, 42, 2012, pp. 123–133.

Langenohl, A., 'Canon and archive', in Erll, A., Nünning, A. (eds.), *A Companion to Cultural Memory Studies*, Berlin/New York: Walter de Gruyter, 2010, pp. 163–172.

Mujica, M., Mayra M., Montilla Peña, L. J., 'Estado de desarrollo de la archivística clásica hasta los años 30 del siglo XX: tres manuales archivísticos de trascendencia universal', *Biblios*, 52, 2013, pp. 43–58.

Rodríguez Díaz, R., 'Los archivos y la Archivística a través de la historia', *Bibliotecas. Anales de Investigación*, 5, 2009, pp. 45–52.

Thomassen, Theo. The development of archival science and its european dimension. In: Ulfsparre, Anna Christina. *The Archivist and the Archival Science: Seminar for 10–11 fev. 1999 at the Swedish National Archives*. Lund (Sweden): Landsarkivets, 1999, pp. 75–83.

6 Postmemory and Ectopic Literature

6.1 Marianne Hirsch: Postmemory

History is a cultural and chronological product of *bios politikos*. History has the potential to disseminate or collect, classify, and transmit facts to future generations. This is a deliberate act – even the ancient Greeks cultivated historical knowledge so that past facts would not be forgotten. The notion of 'authority' was first defined in Rome, and then adopted by the Christian Church to establish dogmatic truth. At the same time, the so-called 'transmutation' of the facts took place in history. This refers to the transmission of events experienced by previous generations to future generations. This experience was often traumatic. Marianne Hirsch, a professor at Columbia University, coined the term 'postmemory' to describe inter- and transgenerational transmission of traumatic knowledge and experience.

Based on a reading of the works of second-generation writers and followers of the visual arts, M. Hirsch notes that historical events have a profound effect on the lives of members of society with cultural and collective trauma (this happened mostly in the 20th century), and based on 'learnt stories, perceived images and manners around him' forms a memory of their future generations. Therefore, this kind of memory is based only on the sense of imagination when a person perceives the continuation of past events in the present. The photography of Art Spiegelman and the study of the Holocaust had a great influence on the formation of M. Hirsch's notion of 'postmemory'. In a footnote of her article, M. Hirsch emphasizes art historian Andrea Lisz, who also used the term 'post-memory' to refer to the photography of Holocaust events. Noteworthy is that the Holocaust is not the only historical trauma in which the notion of postmemory is of great significance. According to M. Hirsch, the phenomenon of intergenerational transmission is also important

DOI: 10.4324/9781003296737-7

in the case of historical conflicts such as slavery in America, the Vietnam War, the so-called Argentina's Dirty War, Apartheid in South Africa, Soviet and Eastern European communist terror, the Armenian and the Cambodian genocides.

Postmemory, as a study of history, is a source of historical truth. A victim of various types of collective trauma creates a part of the historical past. Besides, s/he is not inspired by ideological goals to falsify historical truth. The only difficulty in this case is the time passed since the trauma. The more time has passed since the events, the more mistakes are in the memory, or the facts of subconsciously exaggeration resulted by the pain experienced. A victim considers himself/herself in the middle of a historical event, which can lead to the fragmentation of historical discourse and the violation of dynamism or chronology. When a father tells his child a story that has not been witnessed by the latter, the perception of the story can result in exacerbation or acquiring additional connotations to the event. Besides, noteworthy is that the second generation, who have not personally experienced trauma, may assess the event superficially and less acutely than it was. Therefore, postmemory can become one of the most important instruments for the reconstruction of history, although it has less opportunities for documenting the historical past. The fact that document sources reflecting collective trauma (archives, journals, and diaries of concentration camps) may be physically or deliberately destroyed to cover up the traces of crimes committed against humanity is also noteworthy. In this respect, the participants of past events are an indispensable source for the reconstruction of historical facts. The grandchildren of those who survived will receive information about the Holocaust not from the direct transmission from their ancestors, but from the history textbooks and the exhibited materials dedicated to the topic. This is how trauma becomes a part of memory and culture. Continuing education for future generations is one of the right instruments to avoid possible recurring of traumatic experiences. In addition, we must remember that if a traumatic experience is a part of past epoch, the passage of time obscures the severity of the sensations, and for the third or fourth generation the Holocaust may prove to be a less tragical historical experience. For example, in modern Russia today we can hear conversations about Joseph Stalin, who won World War II and destroyed parasitism in Soviet society. However, most of the victims of Soviet terror are no longer alive, and no one can tell us about the constant suffering and torture of millions of Soviet citizens had to face. On the contrary, the modern Russian government can revive the figure of Stalin and highlight his role in history, which will be based on modern ideological goals. This is the reason for the heterogenous nature of historical discourse, the interpretation of which can be done differently beyond the context. Time changes the historical context and creates the new 'historical truth', which is relevant for modern government.

The works by M. Hirsch made a great contribution to the modern academic research. Her monographs became desk books for researchers in the relevant field.[1]

6.1.1 The Gulag and the Gupvi

Along with the Holocaust, the study of the Main Administration of the Soviet camps is also noteworthy and interesting for modern historical science. This research topic is relevant both in historical and in military-political terms. The attitude of the state toward prisoners-of-war (POWs), as well as the idea of forming new places of deprivation of liberty to place them there and use their physical and professional capacities, was consistent with domestic policy of the country and revealed different sides of the social organization. In general, studies of prisoner-of-war camps shed light on foreign political, economic, ideological, and societal levels of the organization of society, with their strengths and weaknesses, being especially important for understanding complex structural and multilateral totalitarian systems.

The Main Administration of Camps or the Gulag had its facilities throughout the Soviet Union: from the White Sea islands to the Black Sea coast, from the North Polar Circle to the Central Asia valleys, and from Murmansk to Vorkuta and Kazakhstan. The Administration of Soviet Camps, which was established by the Council of People's Commissars of the Soviet Union order dated April 7, 1930, next year received a status of the Main Administration and was referred to as the Gulag. However, the Gulag was not the first punitive organ. There were numerous and different kinds of repressive systems not only in the Soviet era but also prior to it, long before the victory of the proletariat dictatorship.

Anne Applebaum offered a list of the main stages of human history in the introduction of her monumental book on the Gulag, when the exiles of unwanted people were considered as 'obligation to society'. To testify this, she appealed to the examples of ancient Rome and Greek, mentioned Socrates and Ovidius, as well as the experiences of Great Britain, France, and Portugal. In order to

Postmemory and Ectopic Literature   45

accomplish historical and geographical image and to draw near to the Russian reality, let's recall the case of the philosopher and publicist Petr Yakovlevich Chaadayev who was a forced migrant and a house arrestee under constant police supervision. Between the early 17th century and the 20th provincial prison divisions were the predecessor of the camps system. During the Tsarist regime, they were subjected to the Main Administration of Prisons of the Ministry of Justice and were administered with the Provincial Offices of the Ministry of Internal Affairs.[2] A complex and long history of the formation of the Gulag began in 1917. Its point of reference is the February Revolution, 1917, when subsidiary offices of the Ministry of Internal Affairs were abolished, and the Main Administration of Prisons of the Ministry of Justice was renamed as the Main Administration of Detention Places. The functioning of the punitive system was in force and became perfect after the October Revolution. It was getting more and more inhumane forms based on the principles of covering expenditures and new ways of upbringing prisoners. A report prepared by the Society 'Memorial' provides a comprehensive description of the evolution of the places of detention as a system. Therefore, the material is not given in this text. In 1929–1953, approximately 18 million prisoners suffered in the Gulag system, and another 6 million prisoners were exiled in the Kazakh Desert or in the regions of Siberia forest.

In 1940, the Gulag was composed of 53 camps, 425 corrective labor colonies, 50 colonies for minors (In 1935–1940, 155,506 adolescents from 12 to 18 years were kept, 68,927 from them were convicted), 90 children houses (with 4595 children), corrective labor bureaus (with 312,800 persons).[3] In an overview article on Stalin's Gulag, John Keep revises the number of people sentenced to death, to camps, and to exile provided by Zemskov (1989) and Popov (1992) and points the number of more than 18 million repressed individuals taking in consideration Bacon's data.[4] Keep also discusses the death rates of prisoners according to different authors – Zemskov, Dugin, Bacon, Wheatcroft, and Rosefilede – and concludes that the precise number may be discovered in the papers of subordinate Gulag organs.[5]

The Gupvi – Main Administration for Affairs of Prisoners of War and Internees (*Glavnoe Upravlenie po delam Voennoplennykh i Internirovannykh*) was established on September 19, 1939 and after some period, in July 1940 was renamed into Administration for Affairs of Prisoners of War and Internees. In 1945, due to its increased importance, its status was elevated and it was converted into Main Administration with the same functions. With years, the following decrease of status became evidente – first Gupvi was renamed back into UPVI and in 1953 it was liquidated and the prisoners were sent to MGB prisons.

MGB special prisons were organized for those who were thought to be the most dangerous for the Soviet system including own and foreign citizens. They were considered of being 'potential enemies' of the country and were forced to the very hard work, with special and rigorous vigilance.[6] Parts of the repressed Lithuanians were held in MGB special prisons: from 414 prisoners kept in the Aleksandrovskoye, 10 were Lithuanians, from 508 prisoners in Verkhneurals, 21 were also Lithuanians, and from 391 prisoners in Vladimir Special Prison 26 were Lithuanians.[7]

As regards POWs, the camps and hospital systems were formed for them after the Battle of Stalingrad. The best practice of the Gulag system contributed much to this.[8] Between 1941 and 1945, 4377.3 thousand military officers became POWs (more than 580,000 dies). Following the destruction of the Kwantung Army, their number increased by 639,635.[9] According to the documentary sources, there were 72 receptive and distributive centers, more than 500 camps, 214 special hospitals, and 322 camps of repatriation POWs, where more than 4 million POWs and approximately 300 thousand internees got throughout the USSR and other states.

One of the peculiarities of the totalitarian systems is censorship and concealing information. It concerns archival proceedings as well. As a rule, most of the archival fonds are classified as 'Secret' and 'Top Secret' under undemocratic governance that complicates the study of historical and humanitarian issues. The Soviet regime was no exception during which the state archives were not accessible to researchers and a wide range of people concerned. Therefore, it is logically noted in the articles by M. N. Potemkina and A. E. Lubetskoy that it was impossible to study the issue of POWs camps, as well as other scientific facts. The authors emphasized the importance of the research topic and their relevance 'under the criterion of humanity in the modern civilization' and noted several significant Russian and foreign studies related to the issue. The cited article is dedicated to the foreign POWs' life in Chelyabinsk oblast. It is a study of the practical side of the theoretical issue regarding camps. M. A. Orlov's article on the history of the camp #503 in Kemerlovo Oblast is interesting in this respect.

The archive is one of the most important institutions that protect documentary historical information. N. M. Markdorf and

A. A. Dolgoluk emphasized the importance of the archival materials related to the research topic in respect of the reconstruction of historical processes in their article, which is dedicated to the fate of the Russian-Germans. Researchers emphasize the importance of the study of the archival materials for adjoining fields of history, like Museology. Consequently, the issue of free access to archival materials is very important. Both the cited article and V. M. Kirilov's work emphasize that the archival materials in the Russian Federation are not accessible.[10] This issue is so important and at the same time hindering for the historical institutions that V. M. Kirilov emphasizes 'The new stage of the historiography: 2004–2006, in the respect of political repressions'. Similar funds in Georgia including funds of the State Security Committee of the Georgian SSR, the Central Committee of the Communist Party (Bolshevik) of the Georgian SSR, and the Ministry of Internal Affairs of the Georgian SSR are open and fully accessible to researchers.

During the review of a wide range of documents related to the fate of the Russian-Germans, N. M. Markdorf and A. A. Dolgoluk pointed out in the cited article that the archival materials on this issue are preserved in different agencies (the regional archives of the Ministry of Internal Affairs, based on the citizens' residence, Federal Security Service archives) that complicates to put the materials together. We share researchers' views in this respect and deem that studies based on separate regions can contribute much to the reconstruction of the general picture of the POW camps. A specific study of individual POW camps may have scientific significance to restore the entire picture of the organization and management of the camps.

6.2 Tomás Albaladejo: Ectopic Literature

Regarding the formation of the historical past as presented in history textbooks, the role of narrative (the methods of formation of historical discourse by historians) is both evident and complex. The tools, used by researchers to compose the relevant and acceptable story for the present generation, may vary according to the time when this view of history was written. Raw documentary materials, mostly found in archives and other depository sources, need to be transformed into a vital historical discourse acceptable both to the present institutions of power and to the audience at large. In short, this is a method of reconstructing history – and creating national and universal memory – based on the theoretical areas such as epistemology (the epistemological approach makes history part of philosophy, the latter being the intellectual archive for the creation of the historical past),[11] methodology (the chosen methodology defines the approach for the reconstruction of the concrete historical event) and ideology (the epistemological and methodological perspectives are dictated by ideology, as the completed and manufactured story needs to be in accordance with the present political program because 'History is never for itself; it is always for someone.').[12]

But the professional (historical) narration is not the only way in which historical discourse is formed. Different genres of literature play a crucial role in the understanding of historical facts. From this point of view, the cases of literary evidence conditioned by political reasons are of major interest. And one such literary paradigm is ectopic literature.

Edward Said's memoirs *Out of Place* may be a pattern for Ectopic literature. The term was coined by Professor Tomás Albaladejo Mayordomo from the Autonomous University of Madrid. Referring to writers who have moved from their place of birth to another place, Albaladejo distinguishes at least four possibilities of ectopic literature. These are: (1) works written by ectopic writers who maintain their original language in a land whose language is different from theirs: e.g. Richard Zimler's *Guardian of the Dawn*; (2) works written by ectopic writers in the target land's language: e.g. Joseph Conrad's *Under the Western Eyes*; (3) works written by ectopic writers in a third language different both from their original language and from the target land's: e.g. Jonathan Littell's *Les Bienveillantes*; (4) works written by ectopic writers in their own language in a land whose language is the same: e. g. Juan Ramón Jiménez's poetry written in Puerto Rico.

Albaladejo's notion of Ectopic literature was widely received. As the type of literature written outside of its original space, ectopic literature was distinguished from the literature of exile; in particular, literature of exile was considered as a type of ectopic literature with its peculiar characteristics such as the existence of special subsets of exile (exterior and interior), the possible of loss of one's maternal language during exile and the origin of the new literary genres during exile (such as the novel of exile and the novel of concentration camps), meanwhile the ectopic literature is a more broad definition which covers the role of *topos* in the composition of literary works by its nature not only geographical (as in case of exile), but also cultural. The formation of an 'ectopic writer' need not be compulsory phenomenon, as the author can choose whether to transform his/her cultural micro- and macro-cosmos.[13]

David Amezcua Gómez from the CEU San Pablo University (Madrid, Spain) has reflected on Eva Hoffman's book *Lost in Translation. A Life in a New Language* that is a clear example of ectopic literature, or more precisely, of ectopic autobiography. At the same time, Amezcua Gómez considers translation as the key point for the in-depth study of the notion of ectopic literature (2014). In his posterior publications, Professor Amezcua Gómez developed a deeper notion of ectopic literature (2016a, 2016b).

Lucía Hellín Nistal from the Autonomous University of Madrid (Spain) studies *Party im Blitz* by Elias Canetti in the framework of ectopic literature. Noteworthy is that writing in different and diverse ectopic conditions may facilitate the formation of rich, diverse, and complex literary narratives.

Juan A. Rodríguez García from the National University of Distance Education (Madrid, Spain) considered the literary work of Rafa Yáñez as an example of ectopic literature. Yáñez was a writer who never rejected his Galician origin and at the same time was deeply integrated in the new *topos,* where he found himself.

Montserrat Doucet from the Complutense University of Madrid (Spain) used the notion of ectopic literature as a methodological framework to study the history and aesthetics of the *Bilbao Group.*

Jorge Orlando Gallor Guarín from the University of Alicante (Spain) analyzed the El *Diálogo de la lengua* of Juan de Valdés as an ectopic work.

Sandra Mora López from the Autonomous University of Madrid (Spain) studied the notion of ectopic literature from the point of view of Translation and in relation with other notions, such as intercultural literature, deterritorialized literature, and literature of exile.

In 2019, Tomás Albaladejo published an article concerning the present European crisis and the role that literature, together with economic, social, and political factors, can play in its surmounting, indicating the contribution of ectopic literature to the reinforcement of the idea of Europe and Europeanness.

6.3 The Reconstruction of History: Historical Truth, Postmemory and Ectopic Literature

Truth may be defined as the sum of beliefs acceptable for a concrete institution of power. Truth, due to its very nature, may vary from generation to generation, resulting in the creation of national memory. It is extremely surprising to note a dualistic relation between truth and politics: on the one hand, truth is created for political purposes, while, on the other hand, truth in its primordial form is totally unacceptable to institutions of power. Thus, truth is fiction, a revelation made in a certain period, created to please someone (e.g., the government) or transmit personal experience, usually traumatic in origin. From this moment on, there has been a place for narrative (both documentary and literary) in historical discourse.

Acting as the desirable agent for reconstructing past, 'historical truth' creates the present. The political program proclaims that the nation that has suffered millennial difficulties and survived has a future. Thus, the past is necessary for the present not because of objectivity, or to remember what and how something happened, but the sole purpose of revitalizing heroes buried under the dust of archives is to create modern ideologies.

As ideology is a social product, the transformation and diffusion of the reconstructed past are key points to understanding the proper place and historical mission of a nation. Fortified by traditions and beliefs, ideology needs to be accepted in the citizen's long-term memory, related with dogmatic religious truth. The personification of power in one individual is a clear example of political ideology that is observed in totalitarian states. The mutual accordance between state and church has a rich tradition of governing nations. However, this was in gross violation of basic human rights.

Subjectivity is not the only obstacle that hinders the process of creating historical truth. One of the technical obstacles is that the historian selects a fragment from a chronological continuum and interprets it. Taken out of context, one concrete event does not give the whole picture, necessary for a detailed description of the story. In the process of filling the gaps with fiction and imagination, a historian becomes a professional writer with the clear goal of representing their perception of what really occurred.

Bias makes sense when reconstructing history. Without it, the professional motivation of the historian would be lost. A historian may select a concrete period for the investigation to nourish his faith and beliefs. In the case of small nations, studying dissident movements may become necessary to national dignity. Literature of exile reveals the ability to resist dictatorships. The past constructs the present, filling it with meaning.

A historian creates discourse based on two types of information: direct and indirect. The former may be represented by different sources of documentary depositories (such as historical archives, institutions that house manuscripts, museum collections, etc.). The latter, the transition between inter- and trans-generational experience (postmemory), is of literary character (ectopic literature).

In this regard, we suppose that *postmemory* is a type of source which may contain historical truth. Indeed, witnesses of different types of collective trauma have formed part of the historical past and lack ideological motivation to falsify the truth. But here time itself plays a negative role in detailing the narrative. When describing tragedy, trauma, or repressions, victims may forget or hyperbolize what happened. They picture themselves in the very center of the events and thus isolate and fragment the dynamics of historical discourse. When a father transmits his memories to a child, the reception of the story may sharpen the impression of what happened. From another point of view, the second generation, which has no personal traumatic experience, may understand the dramatic features of tragedy very superficially. Hence, *postmemory* is an important tool for reconstructing history, though it still lacks certain possibilities to document the historical past.

As has already been mentioned, history was traditionally linked to rhetoric. The formation of History as a science became possible only after its detachment from rhetoric. Nevertheless, literary aspects were not excluded from historical discourse, and the work of philosophers in History (beginning with Hegel) is an attempt to widen or systemize the work done and the conclusions reached by historian-scientists. From this perspective, literary imagination represents an indivisible part of historical discourse, as it aims to fill documentary gaps.

The role of the imagination in historical discourse became so important that the literary genre – the Realist novel – has been converted into a strong parallel of historical documentary sources. As professional historiography serves the state and is dictated by ideological demands, the literary narrative of historical events (memoirs, autobiographies, diaries of exile, etc.) also has the concrete aim to exaggerate or diminish the role of circumstances in the long chain of historical events. Hence, fact and fiction are two similar modes of transmitting the historical past.

Ectopic literature is a type of narrative that facilitates the understanding of the possible reasons for the creation of historical truth in the works of writers, exiled or not, who decided to create their text in unusual, complex reality. Frequent change in place of residence, as well as of themes, determines the formation of a new type of narrative – Ectopic Literature.

Thus, in coming to a series of conclusions concerning the reconstruction of history, let me offer two illustrations of why understanding the historical past is a complex reality:

1 'For the post-generation as a whole, the Second World War is the great event of that relevant past, the central point of reference, the referent, indeed, for the very idea of "history". The Holocaust is the most harrowing and philosophically pivotal heart of that cataclysm, the part of our larger past with which we have to struggle if we are to grasp something about our twentieth-century legacy, whoever we are' – noted Eva Hoffmann in her monumental *After such knowledge*.[14] Facts deeply rooted in history across generations are mostly of traumatic origin. Genocide is the type of collective trauma that is converted from history into the culture. Time passes and new generations receive historical events as a form of cultural heritage. Documents from concentration camps, e.g., archives, journals, or diaries, may be lost or destroyed; witnesses may survive and pass their memories to the next generation, but after one generation this type of direct sourcing will no longer be possible. And grandchildren receive the Holocaust, for example, as a chapter in a history textbook or at an exhibition. Hence, trauma becomes a memory, forming part of culture. The continuous education of new generations is an important step in reconstructing history. Nevertheless, once the impression has lost its sharpness, it cannot build the foreground of the narrative. And different interpretations of historical truth may appear. In contemporary Russia, we can still read about the Joseph Stalin who won the Second World War and eradicated parasitism from Soviet society. But there are no living witnesses of the Great Terror who can recount in detail the violence against the nation organized and directed by Stalin. Hence, the revitalization of Stalin is important in an ideological framework, omitting the concrete details of Soviet terror. The ideas, illustrated by Antonio Gramsci in his prison notebooks, concerning the transformation of revolutionary impulse by Stalin into an idolization of the totalitarian state, lost their actuality in dominant political discourse.[15] Time changes historical content, creating a new and desirable context for ideological 'truth'.

2 Literature can make a valid contribution to history. Narrative represents the interaction of human beings with their physical, historical, and social world as it (narrative) responds to the necessity of representation of 'concepts, acts and world status'.[16] Different types of historical narratives (epic poetry, novel, novella, or short story) compose the story based on the real facts filled with imagination. The Spanish philosopher María Zambrano, in her essay *Poesía y Revolución* (*Poetry and Revolution*), describes the historical links between politics and literature, in particular the case of three revolutionary activities reflected in French literature.[17] Printing or the orally disseminated word (newspapers, bulletins, speeches pronounced on demonstrations) are useful tools for the diffusion of political ideas. Different human values are spread in society during social cataclysms and political instability. Revolutionary rhetoric is accumulated in memory via literary texts and archival documents. Such historical narrative is exaggerated by nature and the degree reaches its peak during historical reconstruction.

Exiled or ectopic writers compose literature written in a different, extreme mode of composing. Historical facts are interpreted in quite a subjective manner, depending on the concrete context and the knowledge available. Autobiography becomes a fertile ground for giving birth to new ideas, supplied by personal childhood memories. Continuous change of place and work, difficulties with the new cultural ambience and the need to be a part of a forced reality condition the formation of new literary narrative, with different accents and spheres of interests. Here literary discourse interacts with the historical, blurring borders that distinguish one type of discourse from another. A new, hybrid narrative is formed, containing peculiarities of distinct text types and painting reality with bright historical, literary, and psychological inks.

Notes

1 Marianne Hirsch is a professor of comparative literature and gender studies at Columbia University. Her basic works are: *Family Frames: Photography, Narrative and Postmemory* (Cambridge: Harvard University Press, 1997); *Teaching the Representation of the Holocaust* (with Irene Kacandes, New York: Modern Language Association of America, 2004); *Ghosts of Home: The Afterlife of Czernowitz in Jewish Memory* (with Leo Spitzer, Berkeley: University of California Press,

2010); *The Generation of Postmemory: Writing and Visual Culture after the Holocaust* (New York: Columbia University Press, 2012); *Rites of Return: Diaspora Poetics and the Politics of Memory* (with Nancy Miller, New York: Columbia University Press, 2011). Among her recent books are *School Photos in Liquid Time: Reframing Difference* (with Leo Spitzer, Seattle: University of Washington Press, 2020), as well as co-edited volumes: *Women Mobilizing Memory* (New York: Columbia University Press, 2019) and *Imagining Everyday Life: Engagements with Vernacular Photography* (Göttingen: Steidl/ Walter Collection, 2020).
2 Sistema ispravitelno-trudovyh lagerej v sssr (1923–1960), Spravochnik o-vo Memorial, sost. M.B. Smirnov, M. Zvenya, 1998.
3 On this topic, see Zemskov, 1991, pp. 13, 17.
4 On this topic, see Keep, 1997, pp. 97–98.
5 Ibid., pp. 99–100.
6 On this topic, see Iordache, 2019, p. 49.
7 On this topic, see Staveckaite-Notari, 2017, pp. 215–216.
8 On this topic, see Porshneva, Dolinova, 2003, p. 134.
9 Tsarevskaya, T., *Voennoplennye v SSSR 1939–1956: Dokumenty i materialy* (Russian Edition), ed. by M.M. Zagorul'ko, comp. by M.M. Zagorul'ko, S.G. Sidorov, Logos, 2000.
10 On the basis of both the new law on Archival Funds passed in 2004 and mutual order #375/584/352 on accessibility of the files on repressed people passed by the Ministry of Culture, Ministry of Internal Affairs and Federal Security Service on July 25, 2006.
11 Here we can recall the note about the problematic historical relation between knowledge (as the term 'epistemology' is derived from the Greek 'episteme', meaning 'knowledge') and ideology noted by Teun A. van Dijk: '[…] general, sociocultural knowledge, shared by an epistemic community, forms the common ground for all social representations of all (ideological) groups in the community'. However, each group may develop specific group knowledge (e.g., professional, religious, or political knowledge) based on the ideology of the group. This knowledge is called 'knowledge' within the group because it is generally shared, certified, and presupposed to be true. For other groups, such knowledge may of course be called mere belief, superstition, or religion. In other words, beliefs that are taken for granted, commonsense, undisputed, etc. **within** a community, and shared by different ideological groups, are by definition non-ideological **within that community** (van Dijk, 2006, p. 729).
12 On this topic, see Jenkins, 2003, pp. 12 and 21.
13 On this topic, see Luarsabishvili, 2013.
14 On this topic, see Hoffman, 2004, p. 155.
15 See Gramsci, A., Letters from Prison, New York: Columbia University Press, 1994, and Gramsci, A., *Selections from Political Writings, 1910–1920*, London: Lawrence and Wishart, 1977.
16 On this topic, see Aguiar e Silva, 1975, p. 607.
17 On this topic, see Zambrano, 1998, p. 201.

Bibliography

Aguiar e Silva, V. M. De, *Teoría de la literatura*, Madrid: Gredos, 1975.
Albaladejo, T., 'Sobre la literatura ectópica', in Bieniec, A., Lengl, S., Okou, S., Shchyhlebska, N. (eds.), *Rem tene, verba sequentur! Gelebte Interkulturalität. Festsschrift zum 65. Geburstag des Wissenschaftlers und Dichters Carmine/Gino Chiellino*, Dresden: Thelem, 2011, pp. 141–153.
Albaladejo, T., 'European crisis, fragmentation and cohesion: the contribution of ectopic literature to Europeanness', *Journal of European Studies*, 49, 2019, pp. 394–409.
Amezcua Gómez, D., 'La noción de *TERCER PAÍS* en *BORDERLANDS/LA FRONTERA* como metáfora de la escritura transfronteriza de Gloria Anzaldúa', *Actio Nova. Revista de Teoría de la Literatura y Literatura Comparada*, 0, 2016a, pp. 1–18.
Amezcua Gómez, D., 'Literatura ectópica: la traducción como tópos en Out of Place de Edward Said', *Revista académica liLETRAd*, 2, 2016b, pp. 709–715.
Applebaum, A., *Gulag: A History*, New York: Doubleday, 2003.
Arendt, H., *Los orígenes del totalitarismo*, Madrid: Grupo Santillana de Ediciones, 1998.
Curtis, M., *Totalitarianism*, New Brunswick: Transaction Books, 1979.
Doucet, M., 'El Grupo Bilbao: de grupo ectópico y alógrafo a movimiento literario', *RLLCGV*, XXII, 2017, pp. 193–206.
Gallor Guarín, J. O., 'El *Diálogo de la lengua* de Juan de Valdés' como obra ectópica', *Literatura: Teoría, Historia, Crítica*, 22, 1, 2020, pp. 243–270.
González Calleja, E., *Los totalitarismos*, Madrid: Editorial Síntesis, 2012.
Hellín Nistal, L., 'Literatura ectópica: *Party im Blitz* de Elias Canetti', *Tonos Digital: Revista electronica de estudios filológicos*, 28, 2015, pp. 1–32.
Hirsch, M., 'The generation of postmemory', *Poetics Today*, 29, 1, 2008, pp. 103–128.
Hoffman, E., *After Such Knowledge: Memory, History and the Legacy of the Holocaust*, New York: Public Affairs, 2004.
Iordache Cârstea, L., 'El exilio republicano y los campos de concentración Nazis', *Hispania Nova*, 1, 2019, pp. 19–65.
Jenkins, K., *Re-thinking History*, London and New York: Routledge, 2003.
Keep, J., 'Recent writing on Stalin's Gulag: An overview', *Crime, Histoire & Sociétés/Crime, History & Societies*, 1, 2, 1997, pp. 91–112.
Kirillov, V., 'Istoriografiya i metodologiya izucheniya problem istorii politicheskih repressij v sssr', *Ezhegodnik Maiikrn*, 2, 2016, pp. 234–253.
Luarsabishvili, V., 'Literatura ectópica y literatura del exilio: apuntes teóricos', *Castilla. Estudios de Literatura*, 4, 2013, pp. 19–38.
Luarsabishvili, V., 'Reconstructing History: Documentary and Non-Documentary Sources', in Luarsabishvili V. (ed.), *Out of the Prison of*

Memory. Nations and Future, Tbilisi: New Vision University Press, 2020, pp. 153–170.

Luarsabishvili, V. 'Los campos soviéticos para prisioneros de guerra en la RSS de Georgia (1941–1954)', *Cuadernos de Historia Contemporánea*, 43, 2021, pp. 227–252.

Markdorf, N., Dolgolyuk, A., 'Metodika poiska arhivnoj informacii o sudbah rossijskih nemcev', *Ezhegodnik Maiikrn*, 2, 2016, pp. 254–270.

Mora López, S., 'Sobre literatura ectópica y traducción. Concepto y aplicaciones', *Dialogía*, 14, 2020, pp. 268–297.

Orlov, M., 'Kemerovskij lager voennoplennyh i internirovannyh 503–1945–1949-gg.', *Istoricheskie nauki-vestnik kuzbasskogo gosudarstvennogo-tekhnicheskogo universiteta*, 1, 101, 2014, pp. 160–165.

Porshneva, O., Dolinova, M., 'Povsednevnost'plena: inostrannye voennoplennye Vtoroy mirovoy voyvy v Nizhnem Tagile (1943–1944gg.)', *Vestnik Rosciyskogo Universiteta Druzhby Narodov*, Ser.: Istoriya Rossii, 2, 2003.

Potemkina, M., Lyubeckij, A., 'Problemy razmeshcheniya i soderzhaniya inostrannyh voennoplennyh na territorii chelyabinskoj oblasti v 1943–1947gg.', *Problemy istorii, filologii, kultury*, 2, 2017, pp. 159–169.

Rodríguez García, J., 'A obra poética de Rafa Yáñez', *Revista de lenguas y literaturas catalana, gallega y vasca*, 21, 2016, pp. 165–179.

Staveckaite-Notari, R., 'Lithuanians – prisoners of Gulag camps and labour settlements', in Kiss, R., István, S. (eds.), *Gulag-Gupvi: The Soviet Captivity in Europe*, Budapest: Committee of National Remembrance, 2017, pp. 209–219.

Van Dijk, T. A., 'Politics, ideology, and discourse', in Brown, K. (ed.), *The Encyclopedia of language and linguistics*, Oxford; New York: Pergamon Press, 2006, Vol. 9, pp. 728–740.

Zambrano, M., 'Poesía y Revolución', in Zambrano, M. (ed.), *Los intelectuales en el drama de España y escritos de la Guerra civil*, Madrid: Editorial Trotta, 1998, pp. 199–209.

Zemskov, V., 'Gulag (istoriko-sotsiologicheskiy aspekt)', *Sotsiologicheskiye issledovaniya*, 6, 1991, pp. 10–27.

7 History as literature, narrative and practice

7.1 Introduction

One of the most common explanations of history is its characterization as a narration of past events, or the narrative. The narrative is a chronological sequence of historical events and has a definite plot. This definition associates history with literary genres such as Epos and Saga. In the 1960s, historical scientists began to think about possible connections between history and narrative. The ideas related to this issue were published in the journal *History and Theory*. The scientists Walter Bryce Gallie, Louis Mink, Maurice Mandelbaum, and Lawrence Stone emphasized the connection between history and literature. L. Stone discussed the possibility of the return of descriptive, as well as biographical elements in historiography. He opposed the use of the so-called 'scientific (mainly quantitative) and social, structural and historical methods'.

In the 1980s, representatives of French cultural theory brought the issue of narrative to the attention of historians. Among them noteworthy is J. F. Lyotard, who noted that the Western World was in the so-called 'postmodern state', the main characteristic of which is 'disbelief in metanarratives'. Another philosopher who wrote on these issues was Ronald Barthes. He noted that history has developed ways of expressing fiction to illustrate what happened in the past. According to him, historians describe not only the past, but also create it by means of their discourses. The narrative, which derived from fictional sources (like myth and epic), became 'a sign and foundation of reality'. The latter was the result of the realism, which was a literary genre in the 19th century. It gave rise to photography as a social-documentary expression and a realistic novel. R. Barthes' ideas were very important to analyze linguistic validity of historical discourse.

Based on R. Barthes' ideas, historians' views concerning the connections between history and narrative were divided into two.

According to adherents of the traditional approach of research, the use of narrative methods in historiography must be avoided as much as possible. However, postmodernists thought that narrative was evidence that there was no direct connection between historiography and the past.

At present, there is no unanimous agreement on the function of narrative in the process of reconstructing history. In this respect, three approaches can be identified. According to the first one, which is based on the works of Hayden White, history is a branch of literature. According to the second one, authored by Paul Ricoeur, history is a kind of narrative, which is different from imaginary literature but shares some of its principles. Finally, the author of the third one is Michel de Certeau, who discusses history as a type of practice and writing.

7.1 History as Literature

Historians have long argued – which genre history as a science belongs to. While some consider it to be a branch of art, the others believe that history is a scientific discipline. In 1903, in Cambridge, historian John Bagnell Bury noted that history is a science although it is a source for literary imagination and philosophical consideration. He was strongly opposed by historian George Macaulay Trevelyan, who viewed history as a narrative phenomenon. L. Stone emphasized that demographic and quantitative methods have been actively used in historical research since the 1970s. Hayden White, an American researcher in the philosophy of history, opposed these approaches in his work *Metahistory*, which was first published in 1973. Influenced by the ideas of W. B. Gallie and L. Mink, scientific foundations of history were flatly rejected in the abovementioned work, as well as in later published articles by H. White. In his opinion, historiography, by its structure or form, is a branch of literature. The researcher identifies three types of historical sources: annals, chronicles, and history. Annals are the most rudimentary type of them and are almost indistinguishable from the list of events and dates that are not related. Chronicles, which are created by medieval scientists, contain more information about the past and are structurally more perfect, since they focus on a particular subject, e.g., the king's reign. However, chronicles depend on the chronology or the sequence narration of events. Therefore, annals and chronicles don't meet the expectations of history, or there is no connection between narrated events and their historical significance. To create history, the narration reflecting historical events based on real events and with a historical interpretation needs to be restored. According to H. White, there are no events in the past, which must be restored and interpreted because the past does not exist as a finished narrative. Historian creates the narrative sequence of the past, which is called the writing of history.

According to Hayden White, interpretation of history can be achieved through literary means. At first, the historian creates the story of the study period, using various literary genres such as romance, comedy, tragedy, and satire. They correspond to the cultural archetypes that the reader recognizes and distinguishes, for example, romance is the victory of good over evil, satire expresses the primacy of God over human endeavors. Comedy and tragedy are between the abovementioned fields. The first expresses the possibility of co-existence of characters and events. The other expresses the inevitable failure of the characters. H. White considered that all historical narrative is constructed on these archetypes. They can coexist in a certain way (e.g., satirical tragedy). Historian creates the text based on an archetypal story with his interpretation. Therefore, one event can be perceived differently. This can be explained not by using evidence, method, or technique, but the historian's choice to create a different story to describe historical events.

H. White identified two levels of 'conceptualization' to explain the nature of interpretation used in historical research. The first level consists of four approaches. These are: formalistic, organic, mechanical, and contextual. Mechanical discusses historical arguments as defined by laws, like classical Marxism. Formalistic emphasizes the inimitable nature of the event, or on the contrary, certain types include the character of the event (in the case of political history). The second level also consists of four levels. These are: anarchism, conservatism, radicalism, and liberalism. Any ideology has a certain political or ideological position. Consequently, there is a certain relation between the plot, argument, and ideological implication. While in a comic context the organic nature of the argument is used, in the satirical context – contextual and liberal.

H. White believes that unlike the Life Sciences, history does not have its own technical language. Therefore, it uses forms of expression characteristic for imaginary literature, as well as linguistic figures. Historians' work is like to the novelists' work, for the historical narrative is created based on existing space. History is like life – there are no ready stories to be narrated. For this reason, the historian creates historical events himself. Therefore, history is like poetic work, and the categories based on which it acts belong to the literary field. Historical events are not tragic, comic, romantic, or ironic in themselves, but they are created by historians. In addition, every historical event has certain boundaries of the imagination, for example, the Holocaust can only be described through an epic or tragic genre.

H. White's ideas can be examined in two different ways. The good thing about them is that they focus on the historical style of the reconstruction, as well as history as a form of writing, and the connection between history and rhetoric. On the other hand, it is problematic to discuss history in terms of linguistic determinism, according to which, tropes or stories are crucial in the process of reconstruction. However, for followers of H. White's ideas, including Keith Jenkins and Alun Munslow, White's ideas are valuable for historiography to reconstruct the past from ethical, political, or other positions.

7.2 History as Narrative

Paul Ricoeur has always been interested in history, both as process and science. In 1965, he published a work 'History and Truth'. In 1983–1985, it was followed by a three-part thematic sequel, called *Time and Narrative*.

P. Ricoeur's scientific approach is very interesting – he does not oppose or reject chronologically earlier expressed views on the essence and expression methods of history. He tries to take them into account in the process of forming his own ideas. He also discusses the possible connections between history and narrative, which differs from H. White's methodological approaches. According to P. Ricoeur, history is a scientific field. He tries to determine its methodological apparatus. At the same time, the scientist doesn't deny the narrative nature of history. He believes that history is different from fiction because the events described by history are real, and they are not result of the author's imagination. Therefore, P. Ricoeur forms the notion of 'historical truth', which opposes the truth of poetry and the novel. While H. White emphasizes the importance of the tropes in forming historical discourse,[1] P. Ricoeur brings the role of the plot to the front in his late works. The scientist considers the plot to be the unifying space of the individual elements of the discourse, which, at the same time, attaches importance to the historical event.

P. Ricoeur is interested in the narrative as an essential element of communication. The process of self-perception is developed by the transmission of own stories. It also helps to determine the importance of identity and existence. Identity includes not only identity of individuals, but also of societies and nations. Historiography as a science is closely connected to this. P. Ricoeur, like other poststructuralist theorists, acknowledges that the connection between history and the past is enshrouded in mystery, because written history, even in the form of academic historiography, can't describe the past unambiguously. It is caused by the nature of the past – it belongs to time and does not answer to a complete restoration. On the contrary, like other narratives, history is based on mimesis. Within the framework of P. Ricoeur's theory, three types of mimesis are distinguished, which correspond to different stages of perception of the narrative. M_1, or prefiguration, requires the individual to have an ability of practical understanding of words and human actions. M_2, or configuration, is connected to the plot, or to the organization of elements and events, so that created story becomes clear. M_3, or refiguration, enables the narrative to connect with the past. All types of narratives contain these three components. Mimesis enables to create an analog, or metaphorical connection between narrative and reality. Historical narrative can replace the past. Therefore, narrative and history are closely interwoven. However, P. Ricoeur distinguishes history from other types of narrative based on the element of fiction. According to him, the historian describes the real events taking their chronological sequence into account, meanwhile the writer creates and chronologically subsumes fictional events under different groups. Historiography is based on documents and other sources describing past events. In addition, some types of scientific history, including demography, don't use narrative methods of description.

P. Ricoeur shares H. White's view concerning the subordination of historical stories to literary genres. However, he notes that literature also adopts historical narratives, for example, when historical narratives are used to create fictional texts. Some historical events of epoch-making significance may even determine the national identity (e.g., the French Revolution). Finally, history uses a fictitious approach when describing events that carry such ethical significance that historical explanation is not enough to express them. For example, the studies of the Holocaust. One of the purposes of these studies is to form collective memory based on the past trauma.

7.3 History as Practice

In addition to the narrative nature of historical discourse, there are other opposite views in historical science. Among them is Michel de Certeau's view of history as a practice, or as a collection of special actions that distinguish it from other types of intellectual work.

Michel de Certeau doesn't reject the narrative nature of history. According to him, history is a field that deals with text describing past events (including both the creation of text and the study of created texts). Historiography has a vague relation with the real facts of the past due to the knowledge, which are based on the texts. Michel de Certeau finds difficult to accept the realistic nature of historical texts, due to the influences experienced in the process of their creation and, also, for their interpretative nature. In addition, the scientist emphasizes the peculiarity of the literary analysis of the text, which depends on the nature of literature, reduces the critical analysis of the texts, and removes the texts from the events based on which they are created. Therefore, the scientist considers it necessary to find a way between the historical reality and the literary form.

Michel de Certeau does not share H. White's view that history is a literary creation. History, according to him, is a mixture of science and fiction. At the same time, history is a practice, or what historians create using the methodology of the discipline. In his work *The Writing of History*, Michel de Certeau calls the combination of the methods, which creates the history from the past 'Historiographical operation'. It includes three components: place, analytical procedure, and text creation. Thus, historiography is based on institutional context, scientific action, and the writing process. The view that history is a part of a particular place or social-institutional space, distinguishes Michel de Certeau's view from H. White's and P. Ricoeur's views. 'Place', according to Michel de Certeau, has a broad meaning and can mean a university, an academy, an archive, or a space where history is created. In addition, 'place' can mean historiographical school (e.g., The Annales School), or an academic discipline. According to the scientist, historiography should be understood as a collective product and not the work of an individual historian. Social and institutional nature is the invisible cause of the historian's work, which must be reduced for the created knowledge to obtain 'scientific nature'.

Note

1 White, H., *Figural Realism: Studies in the Mimesis Effect*, Baltimore, MD: John Hopkins University Press, 1998.

Bibliography

Barthes, R., 'The discourse of history', in Barthes, R. (ed.), *The Rustle of Language*, Oxford: Blackwell, 1986, pp. 127–140.
Certeau, M. de, *Heterologies: Discourse on the Other*, Manchester: Manchester University Press, 1986.
Certeau, M. de, *The Writing of History*, New York: Columbia University Press, 1988.
Gallie, W. B., *Philosophy and Historical Understanding*, London: Chatto and Windus, 1964.
Jenkins, K., *On "What is History": From Carr and Elton to Rorty and White*, London: Routledge, 1995.
Lyotard, J.-F., *The Postmodern Condition: A Report on Knowledge*, Manchester: Manchester University Press, 1992.
Mandelblaum, M., *The Anatomy of Historical Knowledge*, Baltimore, MD: John Hopkins University Press, 1977.
Mink, L., 'History and fiction as modes of comprehension', *New Literary History*, 1, 1987, pp. 514–558.
Munslow, A., *Deconstructing History*, London: Routledge, 1997.
Simms, K., *Paul Ricoeur*, London: Routledge, 2003.
Stern, F., *The Varieties of History: From Voltaire to the Present*, London: Macmillan, 1970.
Stone, L., 'The revival of narrative', in Stone, L. (ed.), *The Past and the Present*, London: Routledge and Kegan Paul, 1981, pp. 3–24.
White, H., *Metahistory: The Historical Imagination in Nineteenth-Century Europe*, Baltimore, MD: John Hopkins University Press, 1973.
White, H., 'Historical emplotment and the problem of truth', in Friedlander, S. (ed.), *Probing the Limits of Representation*, Cambridge, MA: Harvard University Press, 1992, pp. 37–53.

8 Microhistory

8.1 The Origin and Idea of Microhistorical Approach

Contemporary Italian historian Carlo Ginzburg notes that the term 'microhistory' was first used by the American scientist George R. Stewart in 1959.[1] A few years later, a Mexican researcher, Luis González used the term in the subtitle of his monograph.[2] The author used the term as a synonym of local history. In 1973 and 1982, he published two monographs[3] wherein he distinguished the concept of 'microhistory' from 'petite histoire'. C. Ginzburg himself heard the term from Giovanni Levy in 1977 or 1978. Later, C. Ginzburg, G. Levy, and S. Cerutti began to work on a series of the same title, which was published by a publishing house called 'Einaudi' – 20 volumes, authored by Italian and foreign scientists.

Microhistorical research involves the reduction of the research scale, microscopic analysis of the event, and detailed study of documentary material. In microhistorical research, the research scale is reduced on purpose. This analytical method can be used with events of all dimensions and scales. Its goal is to believe that the microscopic research enables to reveal the characteristics, which remain beyond the scope of macroscopic research.

In microhistorical research, starting point or a research object is a concrete event, which is often very specific and has individual nature, and is not defined as a typical event. It acquires meaning only in its own, peculiar context.

Thus, during microhistorical research, individual characteristics are not neglected to explain the general phenomenon. On the contrary, this method of research allows us to focus and highlight individual features and private or individual events. In addition, microhistorical approach does not imply segregation. It doesn't deny generalization. It aims to describe a general phenomenon based on individual cases.

DOI: 10.4324/9781003296737-9

Microhistory 65

In microhistorical research, history is viewed not as a unified science of events, but as a text constructed from many individual centers. This is no longer history, but stories, or rather stories of historical significance. For the prominent proponents of the Italian microhistorical school, Carlo Ginzburg and Carlo Poni, the basis for removing from macrohistorical concepts and social approaches of history was technological progress and the loss of faith in the socio-political successes caused by it. According to researchers, history as a science should move away from social concepts and return to everyday life, to what people are experiencing day by day.

This approach, which was developed by the aforementioned Italian scientists and their like-minded compatriots, agrees to some extent with the approach developed by their German colleagues. The difference between them is that Italian and German schools are the outcome of two different traditions of thinking. The main representatives of the Italian tradition, including C. Ginzburg, C. Poni, and G. Levy, were at first proponents of Marxist ideas. The change in their views was caused by two reasons – the first was the authoritarian position developed by the existing communist parties, and the second was the loss of faith in the macrohistorical nature that made it impossible to find common ground between Marxist and non-Marxist approaches. Therefore, Italian scientists aimed to highlight the role of man for history, which opposed not only traditional Marxism, but also analytical social sciences. In addition, Italian scientists kept three elements of Marxism historical guides, two of which coincides with the views of German scientists. According to the first element, social inequality is a key feature of any society historically. The second element is the role of production and reproduction in the process of cultural formation. According to scientists, economic characteristics don't enable to explain the social and cultural aspects of life. They become an integral part of them and are an important determinant of social inequality. Although history can't be completely perceived without them, the social inequality goes beyond the political, economic, and social spheres, opposing the Marxist views.

The third element is the belief that historical study should be based on solid methods and empirical analysis. Researchers in microhistory don't share the views of Hayden White and Natalie Davis on the role of facts and fiction in the process of reconstructing history. On the contrary, they think that the research instrument of historians is a real and a concrete fact.

The microhistorical method of research has been criticized for several reasons, including (a) reduction of the research scale leads to a decrease in the scale of historical research, (b) microhistorians romanticize past cultures, (c) microhistorians study relatively stable cultures, which complicates the study of modern and rapidly changeable society, and (d) microhistorical study is less related to political sciences.

8.2 The Microhistory of the Great Terror in Georgian SSR

Let's appeal to a concrete historical example to illustrate the advantages of microhistorical research. According to the Soviet historiography, during the terror of 1937–1938 in the Soviet Union, called the Great Terror by Robert Conquest, criminal proceedings were conducted differently. Comprehensive research of the criminal cases preserved in the Archive of the State Security Committee of the Georgian SSR (present day –Archive of the Ministry of Interior of Georgia) enabled to determine the mechanism based on which thousands of suspects were sentenced to death or sent into a long-term exile. In this regard, many archival cases are interesting, including archival case files #37860 and #38806, which are preserved in fond #6. It turns out, that according to the decree passed by the head, special groups of two investigators were formed to investigate cases. The investigators appealed to different methods of physical and moral violence to make the suspect give up and sign desirable testimonies. This was called 'pre-processing'. The suspects, who were not able to endure the torture, gave fake testimonies, based on which, an investigator made notes on a small piece of paper, which later was transferred to the secretary of B. Z. Kobulov,[4] Milova[5] for further processing and publishing. Three or four days later, the suspect signed a printed testimony, which was taken violently and was called the 'original' by the NKVD.[6]

This example clearly shows the advantages of the microhistorical method of research. It enables, based on an individual case, to determine mechanism by which terror was carried out in the Georgian SSR. In addition, this mechanism enables to describe and study terror as a general historical event. Indeed, based on a comprehensive study of an individual criminal cases, it is possible

Microhistory 67

to draw several conclusions that will characterize and determine the essence of the Great Terror. These conclusions are:

1 Arrest notice was not issued before the suspect was arrested. This was concluded by studying several archival case files, including the file on the head of the Main Division of Resorts of the Georgian SSR Petre Khitarov,[7] the criminal case against the investigator of the Special Department of Transcaucasian Military District Ashot Aslanov,[8] and testimonies of an employee of the Special Department of Transcaucasian Military District Iakob Dudkin.[9]
2 Arrest records were officially made after some time of the imprisonment. This gets known from the file on the director of the Shota Rustaveli Theatre Giorgi Gugunava, who was arrested on the 25th of October. However, his arrest record was made on the 29th of October.[10] A similar incident took place during the arrest of Deputy Director of the Film Industry Trest of the Georgian SSR Ivane Kiknadze. While he was arrested on the 14th of August, an arrest record was made on the 17th of August.[11]
3 In addition to the main charges, the detainees were charged with additional charges. The events like this are described in the files on the head of the Third Department of the NKVD of the Georgian SSR Petre Mkheidze[12] and Secretary of the People's Commissar Alexandre Gamsakhurdia.[13]
4 The interrogations of detainees continued even after the investigation was completed and the cases against them were reviewed by the troika. (In this case, the interrogation protocols were not attached to the investigation case and sent to the archives for storage.)[14]
5. In some cases, the testimony was written not by the investigator, but by the suspect himself, who recorded the text dictated by the investigator. This happened during the investigation of the case against a former employee of the NKVD Mikheil Dzidziguri. Investigator Nikita Krimyan dictated him testimonies.[15]
6 Interrogation protocols were sometimes compiled by investigators who didn't attend the interrogation. This happened in the case of Besarion Chichinadze. His interrogation protocols were compiled by investigator Alexandre Kvlividze.[16]
7 In some cases, arrests were conducted before any information concerning the suspect was obtained. This happened to

deputy chairman of the NKVD I. Stanski. On April 25, 1937, he was arrested based on a certificate signed by an employee of the NKVD Petre Mkheidze. According to the certificate, I. Stanski was arrested based on G. Eliava's testimony. However, G. Eliava was interrogated five days after I. Stanski's arrest on April 30.[17]

8 The detainees were not informed about the completion of the investigation and were not allowed to read the case materials. Later they were informed about the completion of the investigation, but they were not allowed to read the case materials. The certificate was drawn up not on the official blank, according to the established rule, but on plain paper. This fact was acknowledged by repressed investigator Ashot Aslanov.[18]

9 Sometimes suspects 'confessed' a crime after the indictment against them was drawn up, and the trial was held by the troika. This happened during the investigation process of the case against Artashe Avanesyan, who pleaded not guilty during the investigation. However, on May 25, 1938, the indictment against him was drawn up by S. A. Goglidze.[19] On the 14th of June, the case was reviewed by the troika, and A. Avanesiani confessed on the 15th of June.[20]

10 The troika reviewed cases before indictments were drawn up, as it happened to M. Rosenbloom. On February 8, 1938, he was sentenced to death by the troika. The sentence was executed on the 13th of February. The indictment against him was approved on February 11, 1938.[21] The same happened to B. Markovin. On February 8, 1938, he was tried. On February 11, 1938, the indictment against him was approved.[22]

In conclusion, microhistorical research is one of the most important methodological instruments, which can be used for the development of modern historical science to reconstruct historical events and restore the sequence of their characteristics.

Notes

1 On this topic, see Ginzburg, 2010, p. 352.
2 González, V., *Pueblo en Vilo: Microhistoria de San José de Gracia*, México: Centro de Estudios, 1968.
3 González, V., *Invitación a la microhistoria*, México: Secretaría de Educación Pública, 1973; González, V., *Nueva invitación a la microhistoria*, México: Fondo de Cultura Económica, 1982.

4 B. Z. Kobulov – Deputy People's Commissar for Internal Affairs of the Georgian SSR, and Chairman of the Troika.
5 Initials of Milova are not preserved in the archival case file.
6 NKVD – The People's Commissariat for Internal Affairs.
7 MIA Archive, f. 6, #37860, v. 1, pp. 310–314.
8 MIA Archive, f. 6, #5519, v. 2, p. 70.
9 Ibid., v. 4, p. 126.
10 MIA Archive, f. 6, file 37860, v. 1, pp. 337–341.
11 Ibid., pp. 342–343.
12 Ibid., pp. 321–322.
13 Ibid., pp. 330–331.
14 MIA Archive, f. 6, file 5519, v. 1, p. 191.
15 MIA Archive, f. 6, file 37969, v. 4, p. 108.
16 MIA Archive, f. 6, file 37730, v. 2, pp. 210–211.
17 MIA Archive, f. 6, file 37969, v. 4, p. 190.
18 MIA Archive, f. 6, file 5519, v. 2, p. 71.
19 People's Commissar for Internal Affairs of the Georgian SSR, Chairman of the Troika.
20 MIA Archive, f. 6, file 37730, v. 2, p. 136.
21 MIA Archive, f. 6, file 37969, v. 3, p. 61.
22 MIA Archive, f. 6, file 38878, v. 1, p. 70.

Bibliography

Conquest, R., *El gran terror (Las purgas stalinistas de los años treinta)*, Barcelona: Caralt, 1974.

Ginzburg, C., 'Microhistoria: dos o tres cosas que sé de ella', in Ginzburg, C. (ed.), *El hilo y las huellas. Lo verdadero, lo falso, lo ficticio*, Buenos Aires: Fondo de Cultura Económica, 2010, pp. 351–394.

Iggers, G. G., 'From macro- to microhistory: the history of everyday life', in Iggers, G. G. (ed.), *Historiography in the Twentieth Century. From Scientific Objectivity to the Postmodern Challenge*, Hanover: Weslean University Press, 1997, pp. 101–117.

Levi, G., 'On microhistory', in Burke, P. (ed.), *New Perspectives on Historical Writing*, Cambridge: Polity Press, 2001, pp. 97–119.

Luarsabishvili, V., 'A brief history of the Great Terror in Georgia', *Revista de historia actual*, 14–15, 2017, pp. 175–183.

Tushurashvili, O., Luarsabishvili, V., 'The Great Terror in Georgian SSR: documents and reflection', *Annales Universitatis Mariae Curie-Skłodowska*, LXX, 2015, pp. 29–60.

Conclusion

History, as a phenomenon that conveys events of the past, is a field of scientific research, and history, as an explanatory instrument for events of the past, is a science. In the second case, history is created by a historian or a person who is educated in the methodology of history, and who is endowed with special knowledge of both history and its adjacent or related fields. These are: geography as an area where historical events took place, as well as religion and culture as fields that construct consciousness of nations, form their cultural values, and create historical memory, with a collection of its accompanying events that are acceptable or less acceptable to modern society (and thus is doomed to amnesia).

Another field, which is closely related to historical thinking is philosophy. As a related field to history, it can be attractive for the reader interested in history in two respects. The first one is the connection of history with other sciences such as politics, rhetoric, or philosophy of science. It is important to study issues like a common methodological approach between history and the listed sciences on the one hand, and the similarity and differences of ideas, which can simultaneously connect and differentiate history and politics, or history and rhetoric, on the other.

The second view, which brings philosophy closer to history, is the discussion and interpretation of historical ideas in a philosophical context. In other words, to form the foundation to conduct historical research not from historical but a philosophical perspective. If we continue to think in this direction, it may turn out that the boundary between historical and philosophical thinking is very vague or non-existent, or on the contrary – very clear and formed.

The difficulty of historical methodology is that historical materials are not, or are less revisable, observable, or re-analyzable. It is beyond doubt that a historian can restudy the archival documents and reprocess the statistic material. However, the historical context

Conclusion 71

in which this material was created, accumulated, and bound up can't be restored in its original form. Therefore, history remains to some extent a science with a sensory nature, which uses several, and often completely opposite methods to reconstruct the events that took place.

It follows as a logical consequence that it is not surprising that the content of this book is inconsistent. It contains precise approaches like the analysis of archival material and at the same time, narrative research techniques that are based on the historian's imagination and transmission skills. If we add the factor of the historian's subjectivity and bias to this, we can conclude that the restoration of history is a fictional, literary, and politically motivated action.

One interesting reason that forms basis for a subjective study of history is a fragmentary nature of the search. Within the framework of relatively accurate historical study, when a new text created by the historian is not based on a narrative but on an analysis of archival material and statistics, obtained material is never presented in the form of a single complete text. Archival documents are described and classified thematically and chronologically. However, they don't contain the context of the historical period. Historical events are chronologically linked to each other. None of the chroniclers is able to completely describe its modern events because s/he is subjective to the current events. Consequently, if we theoretically assume that a historian working on archival documents concerning a foreign country's history is objective, the material will not allow him/her to restore the historical contexts, in which documentary records and statistics are preserved in the archives.

In addition to the fragmentary nature of preserved materials, working in the archive has another problem. It is interesting what if two or more historians use the same material to conclude different conclusions? How will the 'historical truth' be established in this case? What is the contribution of the comparative method of research to this situation? Or how useful will it be to use a methodology with the opposite nature of research like archival research and history as a narrative, in the process of reconstructing history?

At present no one argues that source knowledge is an effective method to restore history. A comparative study of texts preserved in different languages can be useful to calculate the arithmetic mean and to determine the historical facts with more or less accuracy. However, it should be noted that authors often created sources in their native language, or described their own history, and therefore it is difficult to exclude the possibility of professional bias of the chronicler.

One of the methods to solve this problem is to study the history of one country or nation in a common context, for example, within the framework of neighboring countries or regions. This method may clarify the study of local history, and the history of one nation may be disambiguately based on archival materials or other documents preserved in the neighboring countries. A microhistorical study of events that took place in a particular society may shed light to a general phenomenon. For instance, the study of the regional nature of the Great Terror, which is very significant period in Soviet historiography, may explain the apparatus of terror that was planned by the Soviet supreme authority, and implemented in all united republics. In addition, it is possible to find elements that in some republics, due to ethnic or other factors, occurred differently. This can be used in the research of other related fields of history such as identity, religion, psychology, or other studies.

In general, the comparative method of research is very useful for history as a field of science. Historians compare events, facts, their significance, similar and different natures. Without it, history would be like a chronicle that includes a dry list of dates and events without connections and common content. It is not by chance that the formation of nations as states and the formation of historians as professionals coincide to some extent. Researchers of history compare the history of their own country with the history of another country and use it to express certain advantages or peculiarities. Moreover, increasing the scale of comparison, or shifting the study from local to universal, is important in terms of studying areas such as identity, multiculturalism, and cosmopolitanism, as well as migration and several other interdisciplinary studies. In this respect, it is very interesting to study the history of ideas.

Based on the abovementioned, comparative studies can be divided into two groups: individual and general comparative studies. While the individual comparative study aims to identify local and unique characteristics, general comparative study identifies similarities and differences between cases. The latter has a symmetrical structure, or studies objects equally.

It is interesting to study the related issues that connect history with education. Many philosophical works concerning the aims and objectives of education have been created by representatives of different cultures. In this respect, noteworthy is that the study of concrete or local educational systems, and generalization of their

Conclusion 73

characteristics enable to distinguish elements that will be common to characterize education in general as a science. If one of the main opportunities of education is to understand reality and taking the fact into account that education is a social product, we can conclude that at the same time it is a science that transforms society. In this respect, history is one of the most useful educational instruments, which not only determines cultural values of the concrete historical period that will connect culture with history, but also forms social memory, which will become a foreground for the formation of new cultural values, which will be different from the described ones. Noteworthy is the contribution of history to the process of raising a citizen. The state disseminates and purposely identifies those historical events, which contributes to the connection of the members of society. The other side of this is social amnesia, when society happily forgets historical events that contradict its cultural values. Therefore, for professional success, a historian, in addition to analytical thinking and imagination, needs a lucky star. S/he must form his/her historical narrative in such a way that it can be understood by society, recognize as part of itself, and declare it to be 'historical truth'.

Cultural values, which are the basis of a society, nation, or country, are formed in a specific context of time. In other words, several social and political factors can contribute much to the formation, development, and change of values. During social tensions and political instability, which may change the state order and arrangement through a revolution or democratic method, the established cultural values are reassessed. This is a process of cultural development when one type of culture confronts another type of culture. At this time both are interactive, which is resulted in the creation of a hybrid cultural discourse. In this process, one of the cultures may be affected and even disappear, for example, the Ubykhs. Another example of this is ethno-cleansing, when a quantitatively dominant cultural group physically destroys a small group. In this case, the state creates an icon of the enemy of a small ethnic group to justify its actions. It creates new cultural values, and legal assessment of the event, or recognition of crime are formed because of social amnesia.

Based on the aforementioned, the identity of a society or a nation is formed, because culture, as well as language cannot be developed without interacting with other cultures. Communities will vary depending on how much they will be focused to share their own values with other societies. Like the individual, who can be a philanthropist or misanthropist, a society can establish itself by means of partial isolation or full share of its values, which is resulted in xenophilia or xenophobia. One of these choices, cultivated in historical period, of xenophilic or xenophobic traditions, which have been developed over centuries, will contribute much to the openness and development of society, and make exotic (detached) or cosmopolitan (generalized) communication system of it.

Both research and teaching of history will become an important instrument in the process of forming a modern society. During historical research, a historian creates a new narrative with some preconceived notions. The historian, as a professional and member of the society, tends to find specific documents in the archives or to describe them in such a way that his/her new historical narrative is consistent with the dominant state ideology. For example, during the interpretation of the archival documents concerning the National Liberation Movement, a historian focuses on inner ethnic conflicts, but a foreign historian, who doesn't describe the history of his/her own country, emphasizes the development of nationalism to small ethnic groups within the National Liberation Movement. This cultural affiliation leads to a certain bias – the historian is ready to restore history objectively, based on his/her cultural values.

The study of ideas has a great perspective in the historical context: an idea is an action that is carried out within specific circumstances, for a specific purpose. Therefore, there can't be 'eternal ideas', as the Spanish philosopher José Ortega y Gasset states. According to him, every idea is connected to a specific event, or situation in a specific time, which determines, develops, and temporarily forms it. For this reason, it is important to study history based on the study of ideas – ideas reflect circumstances, and the unity of circumstances in each time is a history. The change of the historical context will inevitably lead to a change of ideas (values, inclinations, imaginations, etc.), which will be determined by the length of time that we call the epoch. While ideas conceived by one epoch will have one nature, they will be different from ideas conceived by the following epoch.

Ideas have a repetitive or receptive nature. If we take another look at the content of this book, we will find that the ideas of different groups are nourished by each other – there are chronological and semantic connections between the ideas. This does not mean that one type of idea is the origin of another one. Ideas, as an expression of human action, develop during a change of action. An example of this is the difference between revolutionary, pre- and post-revolutionary ideas. If we analyze the structure of these three types of ideas, we will find out that pre-revolutionary ideas are boldly different from the revolutionary ideas, but very similar to the post-revolutionary ones. It is a paradox, but the fact is that the revolutionary ideology is a transitional stage for the return of ideas to their past form. Thus, we can conclude that human thinking has a very low degree of mutation, or the content of ideas does not change, but they acquire a temporarily new content, to regain their previous content after some time.

Based on this, I proposed the *theory of interideity,* according to which, every idea may consist of two – changeable and changeless parts. While the changeless part is a foreground on which the content of the idea is based, the changeable part determines the development of the idea in a certain historical context. Noteworthy is that the acceptance of ideas or the development of one idea from another has been expressed in special literature many times: Socrates and Plato can be considered the authors of many primary ideas. Their ideas were based on pre-Socratic philosophy. Since Plato tried to turn philosophy into literature, several philosophical ideas have become the property of literature, and further evolution took place in fictional texts. According to Descartes, if we are interested in studying the historical evolution of ideas, it is necessary to reveal their original meanings.

I think that a concrete content of the idea within the given discourse is less important for the history of the development of thinking. On the contrary, the first content of the idea or the starting point from which it enters the new discourse is valuable. At the same time, the temporal form, which idea acquires, is important in given context to study a concrete discourse. This is the difference between the changeable and changeless meanings of idea.

I hope that this methodological book will be useful for researchers interested in the study of history and related fields and will prepare a fertile ground for planning and implementing new multidisciplinary research.

Bibliography

Berger, S., 'Comparative history', in Berger, S., Feldner, H., Passmore, K. (eds.), *Writing History. Theory and Practice,* New York: Arnold, 2003, pp. 161–179.

Colli, G., *El nacimiento de la filosofía,* Barcelona: Tusquets Editores, 2009.

Descartes, *Discurso del método. Meditaciones metafísicas,* Madrid: Espasa-Calpe, 1970.

Halbwachs, M., *On Collective Memory*, Chicago, IL and London: The University of Chicago Press, 1992.

Luarsabishvili, V., 'Sobre teoría de interideidad (La sucesión de las ideas o del Romanticismo al Existencialismo)', *Aufklärung, Revista de Filosofía,* 2, 2016, pp. 43–54.

Ortega y Gasset, J., 'No hay propiamente "Historia de las ideas"', in Ortega y Gasset, J. (ed.), *Obras Completas*, VI, Madrid: Alianza Editorial, 1983, pp. 388–393.

Solana Dueso, J., 'La filosofía griega en el siglo XXI', *Daímon. Revista Internacional de Filosofía,* 50, 2010, pp. 169–178.

Whitehead, A., *Process and Reality,* New York: Macmillan, 1957.

Index

Albaladejo, Tomás 42, 47–48
Althusser, Louis 24–25
Annales School 62
Apartheid 43
Applebaum, Anne 44
archives 33, 36–37, 43, 47; as an *institution of active* memory 39; historical and political 37–38, 51; primary and secondary documents 38
Archival studies 36–37
Arendt, Hannah 37
Armenian Genocide 27, 43
Assmann, Jan 28

Bachelard, Gaston 24
Barthes, Roland 57
Bergson, Henri 30
bias 50
Billig, Michael 28
Bloch, Marc 14; *see also* New History
Bourdieu, Pierre 24–25
Bodin, Jean 8
Bury, John Bagnell 58
Butler, Judith 26

Cambodian genocide 43
camps: concentration 43; prisoner-of-war 44, 47
Canguilhem, Georges 24
Certeau, Michel de 58, 62
Cerutti, Simona 64
Chaadayev, Petr Yakovlevich 45
Chladni, Johann Martin 28
Cixous, Hélène 26
classical mechanics 6

Collingwood, Robin Georg 11
Conquest, Robert 66
consciousness 16

Davis, Natalie Zemon 65
Derrida, Jacques 25, 37
Dilthey, Wilhelm 12
Dirty War 43
discourse: economic 25; historical 15–16, 20, 44, 47, 51, 57, 60; literary 53; political 16; psychological 25
Droysen, Gustav Johann 8, 11–12
Douglas, Mary 24
Durkheim, Émile 14, 30

ectopic: literature 42, 47–48, 49, 51–52; writer 48
Empiricism 9
'enemy syndrome' 34
epistemology 48

Febvre, Lucien 14; *see also* New History
Foucault, Michel 11, 24–25, 37

Gadamer, Hans-Georg 12
Gallie, Walter Bryce 57–58
Geary, Patrick 27
Geertz, Clifford 24
German Historical School 8
Ginzburg, Carlo 64
González, Luis 64
Gramsci, Antonio 52
Great Terror 52
Gulag (Main Administration of Camps) 27, 44

Index

Gupvi (Main Administration for Affairs of Prisoners of War and Internees) 45

Halbwachs, Maurice 30–32
Hegel, Georg Wilhelm Friedrich 10–12, 16, 51
Hegelian Marxism 23
Hirsch, Marianne 42
historian: bias 7; objectivity 7
historical: documents 37; empiricism 10; epistemology 9; event 60; 'fact' 20–21; facts 16; 'individuals' 21; methodology 9; methods 7; 'reality' 20–21; reconstruction 6, 16, 43, 49–50; representation 15; 'truth' 20–21, 27, 33, 43–44; 49–50
historicism 10, 23; Hegelian philosophical historicism 10
historiography 16, 51, 58, 60
Holocaust 11, 27, 42–44, 52, 60–61
humanism 10, 23
Humanities 6, 15
Huyssen, Andreas 27

identity 27
ideology 7, 16, 24, 48
Ingrao, Charles 37
intergenerational transmission 42; *see also* postmemory

Jacobson, Roman 23
Jenkins, Keith 20, 60

Keep, John 45
Koselleck, Reinhart 29

LaCapra, Dominick 25
Lamprecht, Karl 14
Le Goff, Jacques 13
Levi, Giovanni 64
Lévi-Strauss, Claude 23–24
Life Sciences 6, 15, 59
Lyotard, Jean-François 57

Mandelbaum, Maurice 57
Marx 7
Marxist theory 17, 23–24

memory: autobiographical 31; collective 27, 29, 31–32, 61; 'communicative' 32; 'cultural' 32, 37; ethnographic 33; individual 28, 31, 33; national 37, 47; social 32, 34; universal 47; *see also* Roth, Guenther
memory studies 27
methodology 6, 48
mimesis 61; *see also* Ricoeur, Paul
Mink, Louis 57–58
Munslow, Alun 60

Namier, Lewis Bernstein 14
Nazi trials 27
novel: of concentration camps 48 (*see also* camps); of exile 48
New History 13
Niebuhr, Barthold Georg 8
Nora, Pierre 13
normative rules 6

Oakeshott, Michael 20; 'contemplative past' 21; 'historical past' 20–21; 'practical past' 20–21
Oexle, Otto Gerhard 32
Ortega y Gasset, José 74

Plumb, John Harold 29
politics 7, 16, 33, 50
Poni, Carlo 65
positivism 10
post-empiricism 15
postmemory 42–43, 49, 51
post-positivism 15
post-structuralism 24–26
prisoner-of-war 44, 46

Rickert, Heinrich 12
Ricoeur, Paul 30, 58, 60–62
Roth, Guenther: history of memory 28; 'memory interests' 28

Said, Edward 48
Saussure, Ferdinand de 25
Schlötzer, Ludwig August 8
social amnesia 32
Society 'Memorial' 45
Sombart, Werner 17

Soviet: citizens 43; regime 39;
　society 43; terror 43
Soviet Georgia 39
Spivak, Gayatri 11
Stalin, Joseph 52
State systems: Fascist and Nazi 39
Stewart, George Rippey 64
Stone, Lawrence 57
structuralism 23–24
subjectivity 15, 16, 50

Tawney, Richard Henry 14
theories: cognitive 7; empirical 10;
　material 8
trauma 43

Trevelyan, George Macaulay 58
Troeltsch, Ernst 17

Van Dijk, Teun 16
Vico, Giambattista 11
Vietnam War 27, 43
Von Ranke, Leopold 8, 10,
　11, 13

Weber, Max 12, 17
White, Hayden 16, 25,
　58–62
Windelband, Wilhelm 12, 13

Zambrano, María 53

For Product Safety Concerns and Information please contact our EU representative GPSR@taylorandfrancis.com
Taylor & Francis Verlag GmbH, Kaufingerstraße 24, 80331 München, Germany

www.ingramcontent.com/pod-product-compliance
Lightning Source LLC
Chambersburg PA
CBHW051759230426
43670CB00012B/2362